The Age of Interdependence

Economic Policy in a
Shrinking World

Michael Stewart

READER IN POLITICAL ECONOMY
UNIVERSITY COLLEGE LONDON

The MIT Press
Cambridge, Massachusetts

First MIT Press edition, 1984

© Michael Stewart, 1983

Library of Congress catalog card number: 83-62248
ISBN 0-262-19225-X

Printed in Great Britain

To the memory of Anna

Contents

Preface

I am grateful to a number of people for their help and encouragement in the writing of this book. Partha Dasgupta, Lynette Kemp and John Spraos provided valuable comments on various sections of the draft, and Frances Stewart on the draft as a whole. If I have not succeeded in incorporating all their suggestions, the fault is mine and not theirs. I am also indebted to Joe Pechman and the Brookings Institution for providing me with the facilities to undertake some of the study on which the book is based.

1 Introduction

This book represents an attempt to put flesh and blood on a simple but important perception. The perception is that when governments make macroeconomic decisions they do so in a thoroughly myopic way. They look at the effects of their decisions on their own country, but not on other countries. They look two or three years ahead, but no further.

This limited horizon—both spatially and temporally—may once have been legitimate, but is so no longer. The world has become much more interdependent, and the decisions made by major industrial countries can have effects around the world. At the same time, man's activities have begun to have a serious effect on the environment: decisions determined solely by the needs of the next few years can impose unwanted and irreversible constraints on future generations.

The aim of the book is to explore the nature of these problems, and to discuss the new directions economic policy will need to take if they are to be effectively tackled.

The plan of the book is as follows. Chapter 2 discusses traditional macroeconomic policy—both Keynesian and monetarist—and two key presumptions on which it is based: that in making their policy decisions, governments are concerned only with the interests of their own citizens; and that these policy decisions relate to no more than the next two or three years.

Chapter 3 briefly documents the growth of interdependence in the world economy over the past ten or fifteen years, with

1

particular reference to the growing importance of international trade and capital flows.

Chapter 4 traces in some detail how fiscal and monetary policies pursued in one country affect key variables in other countries. (This is a relatively technical chapter, and pages 30–40 in particular may be omitted by the general reader prepared to take on trust the fact that *any* macroeconomic decision in one country will have *some* effects on any other country to which it is linked by trade and capital flows.)

Chapter 5 argues that the general consequence of macroeconomic policies which take no account of effects on other countries is, given the attitudes and activities of the world financial community, a deflationary bias in the working of the world economy as a whole; and that this process has recently been intensified by a newly-resurrected and frequently inappropriate hostility to budget deficits.

Chapter 6 examines in some detail the way in which the deflationary bias has operated in a number of OECD countries over the past decade, reinforcing restrictive policies and discouraging expansionary ones.

Chapter 7 discusses two different strategies which countries might adopt in order to avoid the effects of this deflationary bias: de-linking from each other by imposing import and exchange controls; and co-ordinating their macroeconomic policies more closely.

Chapter 8 moves on to consider the temporal dimension, asking whether traditional short-term demand management policies are capable of creating and maintaining full employment in a world in which rapid technological change is eliminating large numbers of existing jobs, and suggesting that among other things there will need to be an increase in the size of the public sector.

Chapter 9 introduces a more fundamental aspect of the time dimension, noting that traditional macroeconomic policy takes no account of the long-term problems of resource depletion and environmental pollution.

Chapter 10 focuses on the energy question, arguing that although there is no prospective difficulty about generating virtually unlimited amounts of energy, existing technologies only permit this to be done in ways that will create increasing risks to the environment.

Chapter 11 examines the prospects for energy conservation, and for the generation of energy in non-polluting ways, and argues that these and other environmental problems can only be solved by radical, internationally co-ordinated action.

Finally, Chapter 12 attempts to pull the various threads of the argument together, discussing the approaches which hold out the best hope of successfully tackling both spatial and temporal problems.

2 Traditional Macroeconomic Policy

Macroeconomic policy, the most important legacy of the Keynesian revolution, is policy designed to influence a country's main economic variables. These can be regarded as the level of output and employment, and hence the rate of unemployment; the rate of inflation; and the rate of growth. In a centrally-planned or command economy these variables may be determined—or purport to be determined—by decision of the central authority. In capitalist or mixed economies of the Western European, North American or Japanese type the situation is more complicated. The level of output and employment will be determined by the level of effective demand—i.e. the expenditure on goods and services of the government, businesses, households and (in the case of exports) foreigners. The level of output and the rate of unemployment, together with the associated return on capital, are likely to be major determinants of the level of investment, itself an important determinant of the rate of growth of the economy. The balance of payments on current account will be heavily influenced by the level of effective demand in the economy. Even inflation, though nowadays clearly not simply the consequence of an excessive pressure of demand in the economy, and thus not susceptible to treatment by demand management alone, will be affected by what is happening to the level of demand.

This emphasis on the management of demand as the central feature of macroeconomic policy in no way detracts from the importance, in improving the performance of the economy, of the microeconomic or 'supply-side' measures of which a good deal has been heard in recent years. In Britain, for example, numerous steps could in principle be taken which would permit the level of output to be higher, the unemployment rate to be lower and, in all probability, the underlying growth rate of the economy to be increased. Such steps might include the provision of more effective facilities for training and re-training; increased subsidies for research and development; measures to discourage restrictive practices in industry and the professions; changes in housing policies so as to promote the geographical mobility of labour; changes in the structure of the tax and social security system so as to reduce effective marginal tax rates at both the top and the bottom of the scale; and many others. But supply-side policies of this kind, valuable—often essential—though they may be in promoting a more efficient economy, can in no way be a substitute for macroeconomic policy and its concern with the level and pattern of effective demand in the economy.

The essence of Keynesian macroeconomic policy is the use by government of a variety of instruments—fiscal policy, monetary policy, exchange rate policy—in order to achieve its economic objectives. These instruments will usually have their effects on the main economic variables by changing the level and pattern of effective demand; though in the case of one important instrument of macroeconomic policy—incomes policy—the effect on the target variable—the rate of inflation—is intended to be direct.

In employing various instruments in order to achieve their main economic objectives, governments face three different kinds of problem. First, there is the need for reasonably accurate forecasts of what is likely to happen in the economy over the next two or three years on the basis of existing policies. Without such information, the government is working in the dark: it has no basis for deciding whether, or how, to use the instruments at its disposal. Although forecasting is now carried out with the assistance of very sophisticated econometric models, the economy is so complex and the occurrence of major and minor shocks to the system so inherently unpredict-able that there will always be a considerable degree of uncertainty about the behaviour of the economy even in the short run, and hence about the appropriate action for the government to take.

The second kind of problem lies in the fact that the achievement of one economic objective may conflict with the achievement of another, or may be constrained by other factors. One example of this is the conflict that is often said to exist between inflation and unemployment. Few would now argue—as some did twenty years ago[1]—that there is a close and predictable trade-off between these two variables. Nevertheless, the notion that a low unemployment rate, associated with a tight labour market and a seller's product market, is likely to lead to a faster rise in wages and prices than is a high unemployment rate, slack labour markets and a general difficulty in selling goods, is supported by both historical experience and common sense. There is accordingly likely to be some conflict between the objectives of low unemployment and low inflation, though the parameters of the conflict may vary widely at different times and places.

A different example of the same kind of problem that faces governments in formulating macroeconomic policies arises if a high rate of growth requires—as it often seems to—a high proportion of the gross domestic product (GDP) to be devoted to investment. This calls for either a sacrifice of current consumption (public or private)—broadly speaking the so-lution adopted by the centrally-planned economies of the Soviet Union and Eastern Europe; or a balance of payments deficit financed by borrowing abroad—broadly speaking the solution followed by developing countries. The first course can lead to acute internal discontent, the second to mounting overseas debt-service difficulties.

A second set of problems confronting governments in the formulation of economic policy, then, is that greater success in achieving one economic objective may have to be balanced against the costs of less success in achieving another, or in terms of strains of other kinds set up in the system. An obsessive concern with any one objective of policy—whether it be inflation, unemployment or growth—is likely to lead to trouble. In this field, as in others, the task of government is to strike compromises between conflicting objectives, and reconcile the often incompatible aims and interests of different groups in society.

The third set of problems is more technical, and arises from the fact that the instruments of economic policy tend to affect more than one target variable, or—to put it the other way round—that target variables are affected by more than one instrument. Thus particular objectives can be attained by different combinations of instruments; and different combinations of instruments will have different effects on other objectives. An anti-inflationary policy which relies exclusively on a reduction in the level of demand through fiscal and monetary policy, for example, may involve a higher rate of unemployment, for any given reduction in the inflation rate, than if some reliance is also placed on an incomes policy. Similarly, a rise in output and employment brought about by a reduction in the exchange rate which raises exports and reduces imports may be associated with more inflation than an equivalent expansion of output and employment achieved by a reduction in indirect taxes; but the effect on investment, and hence on the growth rate, of a rise in export demand and a stronger balance of payments may be more favourable.

The art of successful macroeconomic policy-making lies in using the different instruments available to the government in a combination which secures the most acceptable mix of objectives that can be attained. The trade-offs between different objectives will vary at different times and in different places, as will the coefficients which link instruments to target variables; and knowledge of what these trade-offs and coefficients are will always be far from perfect. The essential nature of Keynesian economic policy-making will, however, remain the same. Governments will endeavour to influence the level and pattern of demand so as to maintain output at a high level—high enough to preserve full employment, though not so high as to create inflationary shortages in the markets for goods or labour. Incomes policies may be used to moderate cost-inflation. The high level of output, employment and capacity utilisation (supplemented perhaps by subsidies or tax allowances) should provide business with an incentive to invest, and from this new investment, coupled with other, less tangible, factors will spring sustainable economic growth.

*

During the 1960s, some doubts began to be expressed about the efficacy of Keynesian macroeconomic policies. This applied particularly in Britain—the country in which the *General Theory* had been written and in which, in the famous 1944 White Paper on *Employment Policy*, the government's responsibility for managing effective demand so as to maintain full employment had first been explicitly recognised. One observer suggested that Britain had had full employment since the war not because of Keynesian demand management policies, but because of the buoyant behaviour of exports and private investment—two categories of expenditure over which the government had little or no control.[2] Another argued that because of a failure to understand the structure of time-lags in the economic system, government macroeconomic policy in Britain had sometimes exacerbated rather than smoothed out cyclical fluctuations, and thus been destabilising rather than stabilising.[3] These comments, though disturbing to the conventional wisdom according to which Keynesian policies had been followed since the war, and had worked, were nevertheless made from within a Keynesian framework of reference. The fact that expansionary Keynesian policies to stimulate demand might not in practice have been needed in Britain in the 1950s and early 1960s carried no implication that they might not be needed in the future. Similarly, the fact that macroeconomic intervention might in practice have been destabilising carried no implication that this was inevitable; and indeed there was evidence that Britain was the only one among a number of OECD countries[4] in which interventionist policies had been destabilising rather than stabilising, and that in these other countries Keynesian policies had been successful in maintaining a high and stable level of economic activity.[5]

In the 1970s something quite different happened: the whole concept of interventionist macroeconomic policy came under attack. By the early 1980s the rationale of the economic policies being pursued by the Thatcher government in Britain, the

Reagan Administration in the US, and—though in a more muted way—a number of other OECD governments, was totally different from what it had been twenty years earlier.

The basic reason for this dramatic change lay in the re-emergence of the belief—almost universally accepted in the nineteenth century—that the economy, if left to itself, is self-stabilising. There are, according to this doctrine, powerful forces at work which ensure, in the wake of any shocks impinging on the system, that the economy is brought back fairly quickly and smoothly to full employment equilibrium. Any attempt to improve on this process by macroeconomic intervention is likely to do more harm than good.

This doctrine is fundamentally anti-Keynesian. The central tenet of Keynes' *General Theory* is that the economy can get stuck for a long time at an equilibrium involving a high level of unemployment, and that only government intervention to increase effective demand will set in motion forces which will bring the economy back to full employment. More generally, Keynesian economists have stressed the importance of de-stabilising elements in the economy, and the cumulative forces which come into play once the economy starts moving away from equilibrium, driving it towards the extremes of depression or rapid inflation. These forces—they argue—are often more powerful and more persistent than the forces which automatically encourage stability in the economy.

The main anti-Keynesian, or monetarist, view of how the economy works, which became increasing widely-held during the 1970s, is associated particularly with the name of Milton Friedman. According to Friedman, the economy, if left to itself, will gravitate towards its 'natural' rate of unemployment. At this natural rate of unemployment—which may vary at different times and in different countries, depending on institutions, attitudes, the structure of labour markets etc.—the inflation rate will be stable. Macroeconomic policies designed to increase effective demand and thus to reduce unemployment below this natural rate may be successful in the short run, but only at the cost of increasing the rate of inflation. This increase in the rate of inflation will soon result in unemployment moving back up to (or temporarily above) the natural rate; any attempt to frustrate this process by further injections of purchasing power to increase effective demand will merely lead to a further acceleration in the inflation rate. In other words, only in the short run can macroeconomic policies affect *real* magnitudes, such as the level of output or the rate of unemployment; in the longer run all they can do is affect the rate of inflation. (Indeed the 'rational expectations' school of economists, from whom much was also heard during the 1970s, claims that not even in the short run can macroeconomic policies affect real economic variables.) It is therefore misguided to use fiscal policy (variations in the budget balance) or monetary policy (changes in the money supply or interest rates) in a Keynesian way, as discretionary instruments of economic policy designed to maintain or restore full employment. Fiscal policy should be confined to raising enough taxation to pay for whatever level of public expenditure the government is committed to—i.e. balancing the budget. Monetary policy should recognise that over time there is a close correlation between the growth of the money supply and the growth of the *money* GDP, and should be confined to ensuring that the money supply grows steadily, and in line with the trend growth of the country's *real* GDP. The result of this will be a stable price level, or a zero inflation rate. So much importance is attached by some supporters of monetarism to the balancing of the budget and the control of the money supply that they advocate removing decisions on these matters from the hands of governments. A powerful movement developed in the United State in the 1970s in favour of amending the Constitution to exclude the possibility of unbalanced federal budgets; and in Britain it has been suggested that the control of the money supply be vested in a permanent, unsackable Currency Commission.[6]

Three things need to be said about this doctrine that the economy is self-stabilising, that macroeconomic intervention does more harm than good, and that governments should confine themselves to balancing the budget and controlling the money supply.

First, it simply does not appear to be the case that advanced industrial economies are self-stabilising, at any rate in a time scale shorter than a decade or two. The heavy unemployment which persisted in Britain throughout virtually the entire interwar period, the great world depression of the 1930s, and even the more recent recessions of the mid-1970s and early 1980s, cannot easily be reconciled with such a doctrine. Nor can the observed fact that government action to increase or reduce effective demand does have effects on output and employment. These effects, moreover—because of the interaction which takes place between the level of output and the level of investment—can in turn have a significant influence on the longer-term growth of the economy.

Secondly, even if it is true that the economy is self-stabilising and intervention is pointless or even harmful, politicians do not behave as if it is true. Politicians—even conservative politicians—live and operate in the short run; every four or five years they have to face the electorate. President Nixon, for example, took office in the United States at the beginning of 1969 pledged 'to balance the Federal budget so that you can balance the family budget' and to stop inflation by cutting back the increase in the money supply. Two years later, however, after congressional mid-term elections which were widely interpreted as an adverse judgment on his economic policies and the rising unemployment to which they had led, Nixon had dramatically changed direction: taxes were cut, public expenditure increased, the money supply was rising fast and interest rates were falling. A little later on a formal incomes policy was introduced. Not surprisingly, in view of all this, Nixon described himself, early in 1971, as 'now a Keynesian'. A decade later, something similar happened to Ronald Reagan, the most conservative American president for fifty years, elected in November 1980 on a pledge to balance the federal budget by 1983–84 and to endorse the Federal Reserve Board's policy of tight control of the money supply. By the time of the mid-term elections two years later all talk of balancing the budget had been abandoned, and heavy pressure had successfully been brought to bear on the Federal Reserve Board—formally independent of the Administration, though not of Congress,[7] and itself increasingly worried by falling output, rising unemployment and bankruptcies and the spectre of defaults by both domestic and foreign borrowers—to ease its monetary policies.

In Britain the story was not very different, at any rate in the early 1970s. Edward Heath took office as Prime Minister in June 1970 on an essentially monetarist platform, but a couple of years later, in response to mounting unemployment, did a complete U-turn, cutting taxation, increasing public expenditure, permitting a rapid rise in the money supply, and introducing a statutory incomes policy. Mrs Thatcher, the next Conservative Prime Minister, who took office in May 1979, was made of sterner stuff, and had conceded relatively little to the critics of her hard-line monetarist policies by the end of 1982—though in fact the money supply had increased significantly faster during the previous three and a half years than she had planned for. But her ability to persist with policies which had led to a fall of some 20 per cent in manufacturing output and a near-trebling of unemployment since she had taken office[8] owed much to two adventitious circumstances: the establishment of a new political party by Labour's right wing—under Britain's first-past-the-post electoral system a completely fatal splitting of the opposition to her government; and the patriotic fervour aroused by the successful military reoccupation of the Falkland Islands, of which Mrs Thatcher was the main beneficiary. It seems likely that it was only the power of these two factors which, in the June 1983 general election, saved the Conservative government from the fate that usually overtakes politicians who continue, in the face of the evidence, to insist that the economy is self-stabilising and that government intervention is unnecessary or harmful.

Thirdly, even if politicians *were* to confine their economic policies to controlling the money supply and balancing the budget, they would still be affecting the economy. In fact, a balanced budget is consistent with a wide range of effects on the economy, depending on the composition of the government's expenditure and revenue.[9] But even if one assumes that a balanced budget does have a neutral impact on the economy, this impact is different from what it would have been if the government had budgeted for a surplus or a deficit. What happens to the economy as a whole depends not only on the balance between government expenditure and government revenue, but also on the balance between private saving and private investment, and between imports and exports. A balanced budget represents only one among a number of possible government macroeconomic stances, and will be appropriate or inappropriate according to the circumstances. Thus in Western industrial countries, in which public expenditure typically accounts for something like two-fifths of GDP, the operations of government affect the main economic variables willy nilly. There is no sense in which governments can abstain from having a macroeconomic policy; the only question is what kind of macroeconomic policy it is. Conservative-inclined politicians may not recognise that a decision to balance the budget is a specific macroeconomic decision, with far more important implications for the country's main economic variables than the 'supply-side' factors they may pay homage to in their speeches; but this failure of recognition does not alter the facts of the matter. The failure for forty years of Molière's *Bourgeois Gentilhomme* to realise that he was speaking prose did not alter the fact that prose was indeed what he was speaking.

The governments of all advanced industrial countries, then, are engaged in the making of macroeconomic policy. This is so whether such policy consists simply of balancing the budget and controlling the money supply, or whether it takes the more elaborate form of using the budget balance as a contra-cyclical device, varying interest rates or the growth of the money supply in response to the perceived strength or weakness of the private and overseas sectors of the economy, operating some form of incomes policy, and intervening in the foreign exchange markets.

*

The macroeconomic policies which have been pursued by the main industrial countries over the past thirty or forty years have very largely been conceived and implemented within the framework of two particular presumptions. As a convenient kind of shorthand these two presumptions can be thought of as relating to the dimension of *space* and the dimension of *time*.

The spatial dimension of macroeconomic policy is an inevitable concomitant of the existence of the nation-state. The government of an independent country in some form represents and is answerable to the citizens or residents of that country. Its economic policies will accordingly be designed to promote the interests of the citizens of that country and not of other countries.[10] Thus the economic variables a government will be concerned with will be the unemployment rate among its own citizens or residents, the rate of increase of the prices paid by its own consumers, and the rate of growth of its own GDP.

To say that a government's economic policies are designed to promote the interests of its own citizens and not the citizens of other countries is not at all the same thing as saying that in formulating its policies it will ignore what is going on outside its own boundaries. The forecasting exercises which underlie macroeconomic decisions will require data on what is happening in the rest of the world as a basis for assessing the prospects for exports or the price of imports; and this will be the more important, the more open the economy in terms of the ratio of exports or imports to the GDP. Another consideration is the constraint imposed on a country's freedom of action in economic policy-making by the rules of the international organisations and groupings to which it belongs. The main industrial countries, for example, are prohibited by the rules of the General Agreement on Tariffs and Trade (GATT) from unilaterally imposing restrictions on imports or subsidising exports; and countries which belong to the EEC are constrained in their policy-making in a variety of other ways, though—in the absence so far of substantive progress towards the proposed Economic and Monetary Union—these constraints still relate more to microeconomic policy concerned with such matters as industrial or regional assistance than to macroeconomic policy. A different kind of way in which economic policy-making takes account of conditions in the rest of the world is illustrated by foreign aid programmes of one sort or another. In the early post-war years, for example, the US deliberately assisted in the rebuilding of Western Europe through the provision of Marshall Aid and by permitting other countries to discriminate against the dollar in both capital and current transactions. More generally, all developed countries make some—albeit often exceedingly modest—provision in their budgets for foreign aid.

However none of this alters the basic point, that macroeconomic policy is conducted by individual governments in the interests of their own citizens. Thus the first key presumption of traditional macroeconomic policy is that it is the achievement of satisfactory levels of its own economic variables, not those of other countries, that is the aim of a government's economic policy. Any good or bad effects which the pursuit of this aim may have on other countries—any positive or negative 'externalities' to which its activities may give rise—are no concern of that government and need not be taken into account in formulating the policy.

The second key presumption of traditional macroeconomic policy is that the time-scale with which the policy-makers are concerned is a short one. In the typical case, forecasts are made for eighteen months or two years ahead—three years at most; and the aim is to influence the main economic variables within the same sort of time-scale.

There are good reasons for this. One is that forecasting even a couple of years ahead—a period during which such elements as technology, the capital stock and the labour force can be taken as more or less unchanged—is difficult enough; forecasting developments five, ten or twenty years ahead is generally regarded as too hazardous a process to be of much use. It is true that economic policies are sometimes conducted within the framework of four or five-year national plans of one sort or another; but such plans usually have little effect on the macroeconomic decisions actually made. In Britain, this was true both of the Labour government's 1965 National Plan and the Conservative government's 1979 Medium-Term Financial Strategy; it has been true of France's successive five-year plans, which have been more concerned with infrastructural investment than with macroeconomic decision-making; and, as indicated above, it tends to be true of the four-year plans for balancing the budget regularly announced by incoming American presidents.

A second reason for the short time-scale of macroeconomic policy lies in the short time-horizon of politicians already alluded to above, and the high rate of time preference of many individuals, who prefer—to judge by the high rates of interest implicit in hire purchase agreements and credit card sales—a given amount of consumption in the present to a distinctly larger amount of consumption in the future. If people's concerns are with the short run, it is difficult for economic policy to be concerned with the long run.

This short-term focus of macroeconomic policy does not mean that all microeconomic decisions are also taken without regard to the somewhat longer term. Many major investment projects depend on taking a view of prospects a decade or more ahead, since it can take that long between the decision to construct a new power station, oil refinery, hospital or motorway and the time when the undertaking becomes fully operational. Similar considerations apply to the training of particular categories of highly qualified manpower, such as doctors or airline pilots. All these investment and training decisions require some view to be taken about developments in the economy in the longer term, though this will be more necessary in some cases than others. Accurate forecasts of the demand for electricity in ten years' time, for example, are of critical importance to correct decisions on the construction of new power stations, since electricity cannot for practical purposes be imported or exported; and forecasts of electricity demand require forecasts of the growth of the economy as a whole. Given reasonable international mobility of labour, on the other hand, the consequences of training too many or too few pilots or doctors may be accommodated by compensating errors in other countries.

However although the facts of life may thus decree that numerous microeconomic decisions be made in the light of requirements a decade ahead, there is no such onus on macroeconomic decision-making. Generating capacity or the shape of the motorway network or the output of trained doctors in 1990 may all reflect decisions made in the early 1980s or before; this will not in general be true of the level of output or unemployment in 1990, or the rate of inflation. What is of course true is that the productive potential of the economy in 1990 will to some extent depend on the level of investment during the 1980s, and the degree to which this investment embodies technical progress. Since a reasonable rate of growth—i.e. a rise over time in the productive potential of the economy—is one of the main objectives of macroeconomic policy, it follows that economic policy in the early 1980s cannot be indifferent to the level or nature of investment. But investment in the early 1980s will reflect economic conditions in the early 1980s, and the prospects to which such conditions point, so that attaching importance to investment is not inconsistent with the short-term focus of macroeconomic policy. In any case, the basic point remains: although the potential output of the economy in 1990 will be constrained by decisions in earlier periods, the actual level of output (subject to that constraint), the level of unemployment, the rate of inflation and the balance of payments situation will all be determined by the decisions of the late 1980s. They not only need not, but cannot, be the concern of those formulating economic policy in the early 1980s. Such is the second key presumption that underlies traditional macroeconomic policy.

How far these two basic presumptions of macroeconomic policy—the spatial and the temporal—are reasonable will depend on circumstances. It may be that they were reasonable in the 1940s, when interventionist macroeconomic policies were first being explicitly formulated and operated, but that they are much less so in the 1980s.

In a completely closed economy it is by definition only the domestic economic variables which will be affected by macroeconomic policy: there will be no external effects, positive or negative. In an open economy, macroeconomic policy will have external effects, and the importance of these effects to other countries will depend on the size of the economies concerned, and their degree of openness. The presumption that these external effects can be ignored by the home country may be regarded as a reasonable one so long as they are small; or, if large, so long as the foreign countries regard the effects on them as beneficial rather than harmful. But if the external effects are large and adverse, it will be much less reasonable for the home country to ignore them. The particular danger of doing so is that the foreign countries may react in ways that rebound on the home country, making it more difficult for it to achieve its own economic objectives. The more general danger is that if the home country ignores the adverse effects of its macroeconomic policies on other countries, these other countries will feel free to do the same, and the consequence will be a beggar-myneighbour world in which everyone is worse off than they need be.

The circumstances in which the traditional temporal presumptions of macroeconomic policy would no longer be appropriate involve somewhat different considerations. For one thing, whereas a government may reasonably regard the interests of people in other countries as no concern of its own when formulating its economic policies, the same cannot be said about the interests of its own citizens in ten or twenty years' time. For another, while other countries may react to the external effects of the home country's economic policies in ways that reduce the success of those policies, there is no corresponding way in which the achievement of economic objectives in the present can be jeopardised by any adverse impact of today's policies on the future. Nevertheless, the basic argument is similar. If macroeconomic policies have negative externalities through time—i.e. if decisions made with a view to producing an optimal mix of the key economic variables in a year or two's time have adverse consequences in ten or twenty years' time—then the traditional presumption that macroeconomic policy is concerned only with the short term would no longer be appropriate. The fact that negative externalities through time may not sound the same kind of warning bells as negative externalities in space, and cannot adversely affect economic variables in the present in the same way as action or retaliation by other countries can, does not lessen the importance of these externalities; though it does make it more likely that they will be overlooked in the process of making and implementing macroeconomic policy.

The next chapter provides reasons for supposing that over the past decade or two the importance of spatial externalities has significantly increased or, to put it another way, that the interdependence of the world economy has grown. The question of temporal externalities is taken up again later, in Chapter 8.

3 The Growth of Interdependence

The last ten or fifteen years have witnessed a remarkable growth in what is often referred to as the *interdependence* of the world economy. This chapter briefly discusses and documents those aspects of interdependence most relevant to the argument of this book.

Economic analysis conventionally distinguishes three main ways in which an open economy differs from a closed one: there are inflows and outflows of labour, of goods (and services), and of capital. It is the last two of these which are of most significance in the present context. This is not to deny the importance of international labour migration as a phenomenon of the last few decades. During the 1950s and early 1960s, for example, Britain admitted a sizeable number of immigrants from the new Commonwealth, mainly the West Indies, India and Pakistan. The French withdrawal from Algeria saw a large movement of people of French descent north across the Mediterranean. The German economic miracle was partly fuelled by an influx of 'guestworkers' from the southern European countries; and in Switzerland foreign workers have been estimated to constitute as much as 30 per cent of the labour force. There has been large-scale (mainly illegal) immigration into the United States from Mexico, and the colossal construction projects financed by the first OPEC price increases meant a very large labour inflow into the rich

Gulf states from other parts of the Middle East and from Asia: armies of Korean workers, for example, used to arrive in Saudi Arabia by jumbo jet. These migrations not only swelled the labour force of OECD and OPEC countries; they also gave rise to remittances back to the labour-exporting countries that were of substantial importance to their economies. Remittances to southern European countries grew by more than 30 per cent a year during the 1960s, though slowing down to about 15 per cent a year since the early 1970s; and by the late 1970s remittances to such countries as Egypt, Turkey and Pakistan were equivalent to more than 75 per cent of those countries' merchandise exports.[1] Nevertheless, significant though they have been, neither labour migration nor the growth of migrants' remittances have been major factors in altering the context within which macroeconomic policy is made in the major OECD countries.

A much more important element in the creation of greater interdependence has been the fact that world trade has been growing much faster than world output. Between 1965 and 1978 the exports of developed market economies grew about 80 per cent faster than their industrial production, and nearly twice as fast as their GDP (Table 1). In consequence, the proportion of the GDP of these countries accounted for by exports grew from under 10 per cent in the mid-1960s to more than 15 per cent at the end of the 1970s.[2] This rise was fairly uniform for the main OECD countries (Table 2), with the notable exception of Japan, whose rapid growth of exports

Table 1.   Growth of output and trade *Annual average percentage changes, 1965–78*

	GDP (constant prices)	Industrial production	Volume of exports	Volume of imports
Market economies	4.3	4.8	7.1	7.0
Developed market economies[a]	4.0	4.3	7.7	6.9

Source: UN *Statistical Yearbook*, 1979/80 (United Nations, New York, 1981).
(a) Developed market economies—broadly speaking the OECD countries—account for approximately 80 per cent of the GDP of all market economies.

Table 2. Exports of goods and services as per cent of
GDP

	1965	1970	1975	1978	1979
US	5	6	9	8	9
Japan	11	11	13	11	12
Germany	18	21	25	25	26
UK	20	24	27	29	29
France	14	16	20	21	22

Source: UN *Yearbook of National Accounts Statistics*, 1980,
Vol. II, table 2A.

over the period was matched by an equally rapid growth of
GDP, leaving the share of exports in GDP little changed.[3]
Despite the world recession which set in at the end of the 1970s,
the same process seems to have continued: although OECD
GDP was only 5 or 6 per cent higher in the first half of 1982
than it had been in 1978, the volume of world exports of
manufactures was about 10 per cent higher.[4]

The reasons for the relatively rapid growth of world trade
over the past two or three decades were various. One lay in the
free trade philosophy espoused by the United States—at the
time easily the world's most dominant economic
power—during the wartime discussions on post-war recon-
struction, and enshrined in the General Agreement on Tariffs
and Trade (GATT). In furtherance of the principles of this
Agreement, there has been a series of multilateral negotiations
on the reduction of tariffs and other trade barriers, of which the
most important was probably the Kennedy Round of the mid-
1960s and the most recent the Tokyo Round of the mid-1970s.
The slower growth of the world economy in the later 1970s
prompted the development of—and was to some extent the
consequence of—a series of voluntary restraints on the growth
of trade in particular products and between particular countries, and this process gathered pace with the deepening
recession of the early 1980s. Nevertheless even in 1982 the free
trade edifice constructed in the early post-war years, though
looking increasingly shaky, was still formally intact.

A second factor behind the rapid growth of world trade was

that the two most dynamic economies during the period from roughly the mid-1950s to the mid-1970s—Germany and Japan—enjoyed rapidly rising exports, partly because they seem to have started the period with undervalued exchange rates. Their rising exports financed rising imports, and thus stimulated the growth of world trade as a whole. A third factor lay in the formation of the European Economic Community in the late 1950s, subsequently enlarged in the 1970s by the accession of Britain and a number of other countries; the elimination of most trade barriers within Western Europe stimulated very big increases in internal trade. Another factor has been the growth of multinational corporations. Not only has the proportion of world output accounted for by these corporations increased over the past two or three decades, but their operations have become increasingly integrated on a global scale, so that finished products are often assembled in one country from components manufactured in half a dozen other countries; they are then marketed around the world. Thus the growth of international trade *within* individual multinational corporations has been an important feature of the post-war scene.

Whatever the precise mixture of reasons for the growth in the proportion of the GDP of OECD countries that is represented by exports and imports, the main implication for macroeconomic policy is clear. The level of output and employment in individual countries is now considerably more dependent than it used to be on decisions made by consumers, businesses or governments in other countries—decisions which cannot be much influenced by the home government. By the same token, a greater part of the impact of the policies of the home government will be felt abroad, and a smaller part at home. A decision to expand demand, for example, will have a greater effect in raising output and employment abroad, and a smaller effect in raising them at home, than used to be the case.

The second major respect in which the interdependence of the world economy has increased over the past ten or fifteen years relates to capital flows. This is a complicated story; here we do no more than focus briefly on two aspects of it which are of particular relevance to the argument of this book: the explosion of borrowing and lending across the globe since the early 1970s, and the increase in the mobility of short-term capital.

For a number of reasons, but mainly because of the two oil price increases and the slow growth of the world economy over the past few years, developing countries as a whole have been running large balance of payments deficits on current account. Over the eight years 1975–82, these deficits averaged $60 billion a year, compared with a deficit of only $11 billion in 1970.[5] Although part of these deficits was financed by official development assistance, the bulk was financed by private flows, particularly loans from the international private banking system. In 1982, for example, it has been estimated that of a total current account deficit for developing countries as a whole of about $110 billion, $16 billion was financed by private direct investment by multinational corporations and others, and $56 billion — half the total — by medium and long-term loans from private financial institutions.[6]

The fact that much the greater part of the developing countries' balance of payments deficits has been financed by loans of one sort or another, rather than by grants, has meant a big rise in these countries' external debt not only in absolute terms (from less than $100 billion in 1973 to over $500 billion in 1982) but as a proportion of GDP — from 17 per cent in 1973 to 25 per cent in 1982.[7] But a more immediate problem is that much of this debt has been contracted with the international private banking system on no more than a medium-term (five to ten year) basis, and at interest rates which, in recent years at least, have varied in line with world interest rates. One consequence is that large amounts of debt have now started to mature annually and — since few countries are in a position to redeem the debt — accordingly have to be rolled over or refinanced in a virtually continuous process. Another consequence is that the high interest rates of the early 1980s — the result of restrictive monetary policies in the United States and other OECD countries — have added to the debt burden of developing and other debtor countries.[8] Since these restrictive monetary policies, together with other factors, have also led to a world recession, characterised by stagnant world trade and falling commodity prices, many debtor countries have been hit doubly hard, and consequently have found themselves too short of foreign exchange even to be able to meet the interest payments on their external debt. Thus in a number of cases even interest payments are having to be financed by new loans. This is a dangerous situation. If a debtor country, unable to meet even the interest payments on its debt, were to default—or be declared in default by one of its creditors—the banks which had lent it money would have to write off the loan; and since syndicated country loans often involve hundreds of banks, the number of banks having to write down their assets in this way could be very large. But if one country defaulted, others might be tempted to do the same. For many banks in the western world, the write-down of assets could soon exceed their capital base; in other words they would become technically insolvent. Even the fear that something like this was likely to occur—that High Street banks might refuse to cash people's cheques—could reduce the world financial system to a state of chaos. But there is also danger in precipitate action to try to prevent this from happening. If private banks, in an endeavour to reduce their over-exposure in some developing countries, refuse to go on lending to them, these countries would have to cut back even more savagely on their imports. The consequence would be not only greater hardship for their own citizens, but also lower output and employment in the developed countries.

No doubt it will never happen: the governments and central banks of the main OECD countries are alive to the problem—which is not to say they necessarily have a solution. The fact remains that a combination of increased oil prices, developing country balance of payments deficits, large-scale medium-term loans from the private banking system and deflationary macroeconomic policies in OECD countries have led to a situation in which intolerable economic pressures in some faraway country of which he knows nothing can threaten the savings or livelihood of the citizen of the American small town or English village. It is eloquent testimony to the interdependence of the world economy in the 1980s.

Of even greater relevance to one of the themes of this book, however, is the other side of the coin which has just been examined: the liabilities of the international private banks rather than their assets—their deposits, rather than their loans.

The same processes—notably the oil price increases—which led to large balance of payments deficits for developing countries led to large surpluses for many of the OPEC countries. These surpluses resulted in large deposits being held by the OPEC countries in the international private banks; and it was in a sense the on-lending or re-cycling of these funds by the banks which financed the developing countries' deficits and led to their rising indebtedness. But unlike the loans, which were typically for five or ten years, the deposits were lodged on a three-month, one-month, seven-day or even shorter basis. What matters about this in the present context is not so much that the banks were borrowing short and lending long, since it can be argued that the banking system as a whole is a closed one, and any withdrawal of deposits from one part of the system will lead to a rise in deposits somewhere else.[9] What matters is that there are now very large sums of essentially footloose money in the international financial system which can be rapidly moved from one country or currency to another.

The most arresting evidence of this phenomenon lies in the growth of the Eurocurrency markets. The original Eurodollars were dollars held outside America—at first in Paris and later in London—by countries such as China and Russia, which feared possible confiscation of dollar deposits held in the United States. The Eurodollar market multiplied rapidly during the 1960s, fuelled by the outflows of dollars to finance the US balance of payments deficits associated with the Vietnam war, coupled with the incentive to banks and multinational corporations to hold, lend and borrow dollars in countries free from American banking controls. The 1970s saw a further expansion of the Eurocurrency business, as offshore markets developed in sterling, Deutschmarks, yen and a number of other currencies. By the early 1980s the gross size of the Eurocurrency markets was over $1,500 billion; and even on a net basis—after excluding interbank deposits—the amount involved was approaching $1,000 billion.[10]

The significance of the Eurocurrency markets, which are themselves the beneficiaries of the revolution in communications and data-processing inaugurated by space satellites and computers, is that very large sums of money can very quickly be switched from one country or currency to another in response to actual or anticipated changes in interest rates, exchange rates or economic conditions generally. It is a global market place that never sleeps. The result, as huge amounts of a particular currency are bought or sold, can be big changes in exchange rates in a very short time; or—if a government chooses to intervene in an attempt to prevent exchange rate changes—gains or losses in foreign exchange reserves which can be very large in relation to the initial stock of reserves.

However, the explosive growth of the Eurocurrency markets during the past decade or two should not be allowed to obscure a more traditional factor in the growth of interdependence in the capital markets: the relaxation or elimination of exchange controls. The Eurocurrency system is a mechanism which, among other things, permits non-residents of a country to express lack of confidence in its currency by selling it. Whether a similar freedom of action is available to the country's residents depends on the extent and effectiveness of its exchange controls. Some of the major OECD countries, such as the United States and Germany, have for many years had virtually no foreign exchange controls; others relaxed or eliminated them in the course of the 1970s. Britain was the most notable case in point. In October 1979 exchange controls—which in one form or another had been in operation for forty years—were completely abolished. One consequence of this was a slow but steady build-up in the outflow of long-term capital as pension funds and other institutional and individual investors took increasing advantage of their new freedom to invest abroad: by late 1982 the outflow was running at the substantial figure of some £5 billion a year. Another was that any individual or business could now, with a minimum of delay or formality, convert their ordinary bank deposits into a foreign currency. In theory at least, the quantity of sterling that could be unloaded on the foreign exchange markets was now very large indeed.

*

The facts and figures set out in this chapter can be briefly summarised. Over the past decade or two world trade has risen significantly faster than world output: most OECD countries have experienced a significant increase in the proportion of their GDP represented by exports and imports. In consequence, their output and employment are more dependent than they were on events elsewhere; and their governments' ability to influence key domestic variables has been correspondingly eroded. During the past decade or so, too, international lending and borrowing has grown rapidly, and the mobility of short-term capital has become much greater. One consequence of this has been the erection of a precarious inverted pyramid of international debt; another is the greater vulnerability of a country's exchange rate or foreign exchange reserves to doubts entertained either at home or abroad about the direction of its economic policies.

Some of the implications of this are taken up in the next two chapters.

4 Implications of Greater Interdependence

The increase in spatial interdependence which has occurred during the past ten or fifteen years, and which was briefly documented in Chapter 3, has had a number of implications both for the context within which economic policy actions are taken and for the effects and repercussions of those actions themselves. It seems possible to identify four of these implications as being of particular importance.

First, greater spatial interdependence means that the policy actions of other governments, and developments in other countries generally, will have more effect on the home country. All the home country's main target variables—the level of output and employment, the rate of inflation, the rate of growth—will be more dependent on what happens abroad than they would be with a lesser degree of spatial interdependence.

Secondly, the policy instruments used by the home government to influence its target variables will have a proportionately smaller effect on those variables: whereas in a completely closed economy the whole impact of these instruments will be on domestic variables, the more open the economy, the greater the extent to which the impact will be dissipated abroad.

The third implication of greater spatial interdependence—and for present purposes the most important—is

28

the corollary of the second: home government policy actions will have more effect on the target variables of foreign governments, and will thus play a greater role in determining the extent to which those governments succeed in achieving their desired levels of employment, inflation and growth.

Finally, the response of foreign governments to the effect on their target variables of the initial policy actions of the home government may affect the degree of success of the home government in achieving its targets, and thus require further adjustments of its policy instruments by the home government; it may indeed call into question the wisdom of the home government's original policy actions.

In a general sort of way it is self-evident that the more open an economy is—the greater the freedom of goods, capital and labour to move in and out—the more will developments in that economy be determined by what happens elsewhere. A fall in incomes abroad, for example, will tend to depress output and employment at home, just as a rise in the inflation rate abroad will put upward pressure on the domestic price level. Developments of this kind, if correctly forecast, will be taken into account by the home government in deciding on its policy actions. Less self-evident are the ways in which, and the extent to which, policy actions by the home government affect target variables in other countries, and conceivably cause foreign governments to react in ways which in turn influence the behaviour of target variables at home. Yet with greater spatial interdependence the importance of such linkages has increased, and their nature and extent require close examination. We shall trace in some detail how two particular policy actions taken by a particular government impinge not just on its own target variables but on the target variables of a foreign country with which the home country enjoys an open relationship in terms of trade and capital flows. First, we shall consider an expansionary act of fiscal policy of the kind frequently adopted by OECD countries in the 1960s and early 1970s, and again by France, for example, in 1981–82. Subsequently, we shall look at an act of policy of the kind which became familiar in the later 1970s and early 1980s: action designed to reduce the growth of the money supply. In both cases we shall abstract as far as possible from the operation of expectations and confidence elements, leaving until Chapter 5 the way in which these factors complicate the picture.

Let us start with the case of an open economy in which there is a substantial degree of unemployment and spare capacity, and in which the government decides to use traditional Keynesian policies to expand demand. Suppose therefore that the government administers a fiscal stimulus, either by cutting taxes or by increasing public expenditure, thus incurring a budget deficit, or increasing the size of any existing budget deficit.

Some of the increase in demand in the economy created by the government's action will be met by an increase in domestic output, leading to a rise in employment and incomes at home, and some of it by an increase in imports, leading to a rise in output and employment abroad. The breakdown between increased domestic output and increased imports will depend in a general way on the economy's marginal propensity to import, and more particularly on the form the fiscal stimulus takes. A reduction in indirect taxes on consumer goods, for example, is likely to lead to a bigger rise in imports, and correspondingly smaller rise in domestic output and employment, than if the fiscal stimulus takes the form of increased public expenditure on such items as the construction of roads and hospitals or the employment of more teachers and social workers, since the direct import content of such expenditure is low relative to the direct import content of consumer expenditure on traded goods. Nevertheless, whatever the precise composition of the stimulus to demand, there is a presumption that the more open the economy, the larger will be the proportion of the increase in demand which is met by imports and, correspondingly, the smaller the increase in output and employment at home.

The initial effects of an increase in demand on domestic output and on imports, although very important, represent only part of the consequences of such an increase in demand for both the domestic economy and for countries abroad. (For simplicity of exposition, countries abroad will be lumped together as 'the foreign country' and contrasted with 'the home country'.) Some of these other consequences will now be considered.

The rise in imports will lead to a worsening of the home country's balance of payments on current account, a worsening which will be accentuated by any tendency for home producers to switch sales away from difficult export markets to take advantage of the more buoyant market at home. The deterioration of the balance of payments will also be exacerbated if the increase in output and employment at home leads to a rise in the domestic rate of inflation. Whether or not it will do this is arguable, and in any case will depend considerably on such factors as the size and nature of the stimulus to demand, and the initial degree of unemployment and spare capacity in the economy. It can be argued that the fall in unit costs inherent in a rising degree of capacity utilisation will exercise a dampening effect on the inflation rate; and, more generally, that the rise in living standards made possible by a rising level of output will provide a favourable environment for the operation of a successful anti-inflationary incomes policy.[1] In the absence of special circumstances, however, it seems plausible to suppose that as demand increases in both goods markets and labour markets, prices and wages will rise somewhat more than they otherwise would have done. The same thing will of course happen in the foreign country which supplies the home country with its extra imports, but on the presumption that the rise in demand and output in the foreign country is proportionately smaller in relation to its capacity than it is in the home country, the rise in the inflation rate in the foreign country will also be correspondingly smaller. Thus the net effect will be a relative loss of competitiveness of home country output, and a somewhat bigger rise in imports (and fall in exports) than that which results directly from the stimulus to demand as such, and a correspondingly greater deterioration in the current account.

The effects of this deterioration in the home country's current account will depend on whether the exchange rate between its currency and that of the foreign country is fixed, or whether it floats. If the exchange rate is fixed—as is the case, for example, between the members of the European Monetary System (EMS)—the deterioration in the home country's current account will lead to a fall in its external reserves (net of liabilities). Unless offset by deliberate action on the part of the government, this fall in reserves will lead to a contraction of the monetary base in the home country, and a downward pressure on the money supply and an upward pressure on interest rates, which will go some way to offset the expansionary effects of the original fiscal stimulus. Abroad, there will be effects in the other direction: the improvement in the current account of the foreign country (which is now exporting more to the home country) will lead to a rise in its external reserves which, in the absence of sterilisation measures by the foreign government, will expand the monetary base and hence lead to a tendency for the money supply to expand and interest rates to fall. Thus the upward nudge to output, employment and prices in the foreign country imparted by the initial increase in exports to the home country will be compounded by a subsequent expansion of credit and downward pressure on interest rates, and this, together with the transmission to the internal price level, via the fixed exchange rate, of the rise in prices in the home country, will mean a further boost to inflation in the foreign country.

If, on the other hand, exchange rates are floating—as has been the case with the main currencies or currency-blocs since 1973—the effects on both the home country and the foreign country will be different. The worsening of its current account will cause the currency of the home country to depreciate, leading fairly soon to an increase in the inflation rate as a result of higher import prices, and possibly to a further increase in domestic output and employment as a result of the increase in exports, and dampening effect on imports, to which the fall in the exchange rate may give rise. Any further increase in domestic output and employment will itself tend to increase the inflation rate further. Under a floating exchange rate system, in short—and still abstracting from the operation of confidence factors—the effects of the original stimulus on output, employment and prices in the home country will normally be enhanced: unemployment will fall more, and inflation will rise more, than under a regime of fixed exchange rates.

For the foreign country, under a floating exchange rate system, the effects will be the opposite. The rise in its exports to the home country and the consequent improvement in its current account will lead to some appreciation of its currency, and this in turn will have a downward influence on its inflation rate, via lower import prices, and a downward influence on its output and employment, as a result of a reduction in demand for its—now more expensive—exports. Thus it is clear that the net impact on the foreign country of a stimulus to demand in the home country will be less under a system of floating exchange rates than under a system of fixed exchange rates. the net impact on inflation in the foreign country is indeterminate, since it is possible that the downward pressure on its domestic prices resulting from the appreciation of its currency will more than offset the upward pressure stemming from the higher level of output and employment. The higher level of output and employment, on the other hand, is unlikely to be cancelled out by the decline in exports following the appreciation of the exchange rate, and so a net increase in the level of economic activity, leading to a fall in unemployment, is likely to be the unambiguous consequence in the foreign country of the stimulus to demand in the home country. Nevertheless, this increase will be smaller than under a fixed exchange rate system.

So far, we have been considering the effect on employment and inflation, in both the home country and the foreign country, and under both a fixed rate system and a floating rate system, of a fiscal stimulus administered in the home country. But we have not yet looked at the *further* implications for key variables in both countries of the method chosen to *finance* the fiscal stimulus.

Although in principle a budget deficit created—or increased—by a cut in taxation or increase in public expenditure can be financed by running down foreign exchange reserves or borrowing from abroad, in practice, in OECD countries, the choice normally lies between selling government bonds (gilt-edged securities) to the non-bank private sector, and short-term borrowing from the banking system. Let us first consider what happens when the home government finances its budget deficit (or the increase in its deficit) mainly by sales of gilts to the non-bank private sector—which will be the appropriate thing for it to do if its *monetary* policy focuses on the control or influencing of monetary aggregates rather than on the control or influencing of interest rates.

If the budget deficit is financed mainly by gilt sales, there will be a rise in interest rates, since there is a presumption that the non-bank private sector will only be willing to hold a larger volume of government stock in its portfolio if the yield is increased. This rise in interest rates may have some depressing effect on other kinds of expenditure, particularly private investment.[2] However there is a good deal of empirical evidence which suggests that interest rates as such are a less important factor in private sector investment decisions than the prospects for increased sales, so that the adverse effect on investment of higher interest rates may well be more than offset by the prospect of the rising level of output and employment in the economy to which the government's fiscal stimulus should give rise.

The rise in interest rates resulting from the government's financing its budget deficit by sales of gilts will, however, have a number of other effects which need to be considered. If both the home and the foreign country have open economies in the sense that capital is free to flow in and out, and if, more particularly, financial assets such as government bonds denominated in the home country's currency are regarded as good substitutes for financial assets such as government bonds denominated in the foreign country's currency, then the rise in interest rates in the home country will lead to an influx of capital from the foreign country.[3]

The effects of this influx of capital on both the home country and the foreign country will vary according to whether the exchange rate between the currencies of the two countries is fixed or floating. Under a fixed exchange rate, the inflow of capital from abroad will raise the home country's foreign exchange reserves and lead to an increase in the money supply and downward pressure on interest rates. If the home government, following the logic which impelled it to finance the original fiscal stimulus by sales of gilts, wishes to avoid any significant increase in the money supply, it will need to sterilise this inflow of capital by engaging in open-market operations—selling more government securities to both home and foreign non-bank private sectors. If the government does not sterilise the inflow of capital, the original fiscal stimulus to employment and prices will, in the short run at least, be enhanced by a monetary expansion. Under a floating exchange rate regime, on the other hand, the home country's currency will appreciate as the portfolios of both home and foreign residents are adjusted to take advantage of higher home interest rates. The adverse effect of this on exports and the favourable effect on import prices will have a moderating influence on the rise in employment and prices in the home country prompted by the fiscal stimulus.

The impact on the foreign country of the inflow of capital to the home country in response to the rise in interest rates there will basically be the mirror-image of the impact on the home country. Under a fixed exchange rate system there will be (in the absence of sterilisation by the foreign government) an initial contractionary effect on the foreign country's money supply and an upward impulse to its interest rates. Only in the slightly longer run, as the foreign country's exports rise in response to the increased level of activity in the home country, will this dampening effect on employment and inflation be reversed: as the foreign country moves into balance of payments surplus with the home country, its foreign exchange reserves and money supply will rise, and employment and prices will increase. Under a floating rate system, on the other hand, the outflow of capital from the foreign country to take advantage of the rise in interest rates in the home country will initially cause the foreign country's exchange rate to depreciate, presaging an expansionary effect on its employment and price level. But as the effect of the fiscal stimulus in the home country starts to assert itself, and rising incomes and prices in the home country raise the foreign country's exports further and improve its current account, its exchange rate will appreciate, restraining the growth in its export volume and, by reducing import prices, moderating the rise in its domestic price level. At the end of the day it is likely, though not inevitable, that the upward influence on employment and prices in the foreign country resulting from the expansion of the home economy will be less under a floating exchange rate system than under a fixed rate one: the floating rate will to some extent insulate the foreign economy from the increase in employment and prices in the home economy.

So far we have been considering what happens when the home government finances the increase in its budget deficit by sales of gilt-edged securities to the non-bank private sector. What happens if—because for example it is more concerned to stabilise interest rates than to control the growth of the money supply—it finances the increase in its budget deficit mainly by borrowing from the banking system through sales of short-term Treasury bills?[4] There will be an increase in the monetary base and thus a rise in the money supply and a generally expansionary effect on the economy: the original fiscal stimulus to employment and prices will be augmented. Under a fixed exchange rate system this will lead to a bigger increase in imports and a bigger fall in foreign exchange reserves, which will eventually—if the government does not sterilise the effects of the fall in reserves by open-market purchases of gilts—offset some part of the initial fiscal expansion. Under a fixed exchange rate regime, therefore, financing an increased budget deficit in an open economy by borrowing from the banking system will unambiguously result in a monetary expansion which will, at any rate in the short run, enhance the original fiscal stimulus; whereas how far the original stimulus will be enhanced if it is financed by bond sales will depend on how far the government refrains from sterilising capital inflows attracted by the higher level of interest rates.

Under a floating exchange rate regime, financing a fiscal stimulus mainly by borrowing from the banking system is likely to lead to a fairly rapid fall in the exchange rate, not just because of the expansionary effect on the level of activity resulting from the increase in the money supply, but also because of expectations (fostered particularly by the work of monetarist economists) that a faster rise in the money supply will lead to a faster rate of inflation. This fall in the exchange rate will in turn lead to an increase in the inflation rate, and this may limit the increase in exports and thus the increase in output and employment that a fall in the exchange rate might be expected to promote.

Finally, there is the question of what happens to key variables in the foreign country when fiscal expansion in the home country is financed by short-term borrowing from the banking system. Because, under a fixed exchange rate system, the rise in employment and inflation in the home country will be greater than with bond financing, the foreign country will experience a bigger rise in exports, a bigger increase in its foreign exchange reserves and thus—in the absence of sterilisation measures—in its money supply. Thus, in contrast to what happens when the home country finances its fiscal expansion by sales of gilt-edges securities, the upward impact on employment and prices in the foreign country resulting from the home country's fiscal stimulus will be *augmented* when that stimulus is financed by the sale of Treasury bills to the banking system under a fixed exchange rate regime.

Under a floating exchange rate regime, on the other hand, the foreign country's key variables will to a considerable extent be insulated from the effects of the expansion in the home country. This is because the rising level of output and imports in the home country, together perhaps with fears that the rise in the money supply will increase the inflation rate, will lead to a fall in the home country's exchange rate and thus a rise in the foreign country's exchange rate. This rise in its exchange rate will both moderate the increase in the volume of its exports to the home country, and inhibit the transmission of increases in the price level in the home country to the price level in the foreign country. How the final effects on employment and inflation in the foreign country will compare with what happens when the fiscal expansion in the home country is financed by sales of gilts will vary according to the size of the relevant coefficients. In the case of gilt financing, the rise in incomes and employment in the home country resulting from a given fiscal stimulus is likely to be smaller than in the case of Treasury bill financing, and so, correspondingly, is likely to be the rise in exports from the foreign country. On the other hand, the outflow of capital from the foreign country to take advantage of higher interest rates in the home country in the case of gilt financing will at first depreciate the foreign country's exchange rate, with an upward impact on its exports and import prices. In the case of Treasury bill financing, on the other hand, there will be no initial depreciation—and may even be an appreciation—of the foreign country's exchange rate, and to that extent the expansionary and inflationary impact on the foreign country of the larger rise in employment and prices in the home country will be moderated.

To summarise this section of the argument so far: an

expansionary fiscal action in the home country will almost invariably have some expansionary effect on the foreign country. The effects will differ according to whether the fiscal expansion is financed by bond sales or by increasing the money supply; and generally speaking the expansionary impact on the foreign country will be greater under a fixed exchange rate regime than a floating one. But the crucial point is that the foreign country will find that its key economic variables—output, employment and prices—have been affected, in ways it may or may not welcome, by an expansionary act of fiscal policy in the home country.

Let us now consider—much more briefly—what happens when the home country adopts a policy entirely different from the expansionary fiscal policy discussed above—though one much more familiar in recent years, particularly in Britain and the US: a policy of reducing the rate of growth of the money supply in order to bring down the rate of inflation.

In an advanced industrial economy, in which the bulk of the money supply consists of bank deposits, and in which the banking system has the power to *create* deposits by making loans and advances to its customers, action to reduce the *supply of* money in practice means—at any rate according to Keynesians—action to reduce the *demand for* money. Traditionally, the government sells securities in the open market so as to increase the private sector's holdings of government securities and reduce its holdings of money. The fall in security prices needed to persuade the private sector to adjust its portfolio in this way will imply a rise in interest rates, a process likely to be reinforced by a rise in the Central Bank's discount rate. Whatever the precise combination of techniques employed by the authorities, the result of higher interest rates will be a fall in the demand for money, and hence a reduction in the supply of money. Monetarists are inclined to argue that the Central Bank can procure this result by simply reducing the monetary base—which, looked at from another angle, is the total of the liabilities of the Central Bank to the banking system; in other words they argue that the authorities can control the money supply directly. Whether or not this argument is correct is in any event partly a matter of semantics, and need not detain us here: the important point is that everyone involved in the debate would agree that action to reduce the money supply will, at any rate in the short run, involve a rise in interest rates.

This rise in interest rates will, in itself, have some contractionary effect on the economy, particularly on private investment and sectors such as housing and even cars, where personal expenditure is typically financed by long-term loans. However the contractionary effects on the economy of a policy of reducing the growth of the money supply are unlikely to be confined to the consequences of higher interest rates alone. This is because governments which place a reduction in the growth of the money supply at the centre of their macroeconomic policy usually attach almost equal importance to a reduction in the size of the budget deficit. It is clear from the earlier discussion that there is good reason for this: since one way of financing a budget deficit is by short-term borrowing from the banking system which has the effect of increasing the money supply, there is a presumption that a smaller budget deficit will, at a given level of interest rates, be consistent with a lower rate of growth of the money supply. Thus the Reagan Administration which took office in the US in January 1981 aimed to reduce and finally eliminate the budget deficit over a period of four years; and the Thatcher government which came into power in Britain in May 1979 saw a steady reduction of the budget deficit (the Public Sector Borrowing Requirement, or PSBR) over a four-year period as the main instrument for securing a steady reduction, over the same four-year period, in the rate of growth of the money supply. Because governments with this kind of ideological approach believe in cutting taxes—and both Thatcher and Reagan cut income taxes sharply, particularly at the top of the range, as soon as possible after taking office—reducing the budget deficit requires very large cuts in public expenditure, and the contractionary effect of this on the economy, and the dampening effect on inflation, may be much larger than the contractionary effect of higher interest rates alone.

The impact on any foreign country of action in the home country to reduce the growth of the money supply will depend—just as with action to impart a fiscal stimulus—both on the extent of the freedom with which goods and capital flow between the two countries, and on whether the exchange rate between them is fixed or floating. Under a fixed exchange rate system the contraction of economic activity in the home country will cause the foreign country's exports to fall, and the rise in interest rates in the home country will lead to an outflow of capital from the foreign country which will cause a fall in its foreign exchange reserves and—in the absence of sterilisation—further downward pressure on its employment and inflation rate. Under a floating rate system, on the other hand, the outflow of capital from the foreign country to take advantage of higher interest rates in the home country will depress its exchange rate—a process which may be reinforced if an influx of capital into the home country is fostered not only by the increase in its interest rates, but also by an expectation that the measures to reduce the growth of its money supply will soon lead to a lower inflation rate. This fall in its exchange rate will put upward pressure on the foreign country's internal price level, and this may offset or outweigh any downward effects on inflation resulting from the fall in the volume of exports in response to the contraction of activity in the home country. This fall in exports will in any event be moderated by some fall in the foreign country's exchange rate. Thus it is clear that the downward impact on employment and inflation in the foreign country will be less under a floating than under a fixed exchange rate; indeed it is conceivable, if unlikely, that the size of the various coefficients involved is such as to increase both employment and prices in the foreign country.

*

We have now discussed at some length how an act of fiscal expansion in one country will affect key variables in another country with which it is to some extent interdependent, and, more briefly, how the same thing is true of an act of monetary contraction. Similar effects could be traced in the case of a contractionary fiscal policy in the home country, or an expansionary monetary policy. It is clear that the size of the effect on key variables in the foreign country will depend on whether the exchange rate between the two countries is fixed or floating, and on whether a fiscal expansion or contraction, where that is the policy action taken, has its main effects on interest rates or on the money supply. But it will also depend on a whole host of other variables, such as the relative size of the two economies, the extent of trade between them, their marginal propensity to import, their elasticity of supply of exports, the sensitivity of capital flows to both interest rate differentials and exchange rate expectations, the responsiveness of wages and price to changes in effective demand, and so on. Nevertheless, the point which emerges clearly from the analysis is that regardless of the type of exchange rate regime in existence, and regardless of the size of particular coefficients, *any* fiscal or monetary policy action taken by the home country in order to affect key target variables in the home country will, willy-nilly, have some effect on key target variables in the foreign country. Generally speaking, expansionary policies in the home country will exert some upward influence on output and prices in the foreign country; deflationary policies will exert some downward influence.

These influences may not be unwelcome to the government of the foreign country. It may, for example, have been inhibited from pursuing expansionary policies that it would otherwise have liked to pursue by fears of the balance of payments consequences, with the possibility of an unacceptable loss of reserves under a fixed exchange rate system, or an unacceptable fall in the exchange rate under a floating rate system. In this situation an expansionary fiscal action by the home government would help to solve the foreign government's problem: the foreign country's exports would rise, simultaneously increasing employment and strengthening its balance of payments on current account. The foreign government would welcome this outcome, and take no offsetting action. It might indeed be sufficiently encouraged (under a floating exchange rate system) by the appreciation of its currency and the dampening effect of this on inflation to initiate further expansionary action of its own, with the result that the original expansionary impetus in the home country will be enhanced by the reactions of the foreign country.

However such a reaction on the part of the foreign

government is by no means inevitable. If it is more concerned to curb inflation than to reduce unemployment it may not welcome the consequences of expansionary measures taken by the home country, particularly if exchange rates are fixed and rising prices in the home country are transmitted fairly directly to the price level in the foreign country. In the later 1960s, for example, Germany viewed with grave misgivings the inflationary impulses transmitted to it by the highly expansionary policies being pursued by the United States, and reacted by attempting to sterilise the inflow of capital and by permitting a series of appreciations of the Deutschmark—the latter being one factor that led to the breakdown of the Bretton Woods system in the early 1970s.

Even more unwelcome to the foreign country are likely to be the effects of deflationary monetary policies in the home country. This is especially true if the home country in question is the United States, still far and away the world's biggest economy, and one whose interest rates, in particular, set the tone for interest rates round the world. Under a fixed rate system—where, in the above example, a country's currency is pegged to the dollar—the foreign country will suffer a fall in exports and an outflow of capital which, if it is to protect its reserves, it may need to stem by raising its own interest rates. The effect will be a double dose of deflation. Under a floating rate system the outflow of capital to take advantage of higher interest rates in the home country will cause a fall in the foreign country's exchange rate, and although in itself this will moderate the fall in its exports to the home country, the fear of rising inflation resulting from a falling exchange rate may impel it to raise its own interest rates. This, indeed, is precisely what most OECD countries were forced to do in the early 1980s in the wake of the tight monetary policies adopted in the United States in October 1979, and their intensification after the Reagan Administration took office in January 1981.

However, the story does not end there. The effects of the home country's actions on the foreign country will frequently lead to further repercussions on the home country. To some extent this will happen automatically: deflationary action by the home country, for example, leading to a fall in output and employment in the foreign country, will feed back into lower exports from the home country and thus exert further deflationary pressure there. In some cases it will be the defensive policy reactions of the foreign country that will have this feedback effect. This will happen, for example, when the foreign country, alarmed at the inflationary effects — particularly under a fixed exchange rate system — of expansionary measures in the home country, adopts more restrictive policies, which reduce the home country's exports and thus in some degree negate the expansionary action it has taken.

*

We have now considered four of the implications of the increase in spatial interdependence over the past ten or fifteen years. Policy actions and other developments in foreign countries will have more effect on the home country; the home government's policy instruments will have less effect on its target variables; these instruments will have more effect on foreign governments' target variables; and foreign governments' responses to these effects will in turn have some influence on the home country's target variables. The first two of these changes are, at any rate in principle, taken into account in the major countries' economic decision-making. The structure of forecasting models will reflect, for example, the greater weight of exports in GDP; and governments will attempt to allow for the looser and less certain relationships between their economic instruments and their target variables which are the consequence of the greater openness of their economies. But governments make little or no attempt, even in principle, to take account of the other two changes. They do not try to assess the impact of their decisions on other countries, although this impact may be considerably greater than it was ten or fifteen years ago; nor, *a fortiori*, do they attempt to calculate how foreign governments' reactions to these impacts may in turn rebound on them.

It is not difficult to see why governments are uninterested in the effects of their actions on other countries *per se*. In an ideal world, governments would no doubt take account of the consequences — good or bad — of their decisions for the welfare of everybody affected, regardless of where they happened to live. In the world we actually inhabit, however, it is to the people of their own country alone that governments are answerable, and it is the effects of their policies on them alone that governments are likely to consider. From the point of view of the individual government, this is a perfectly rational thing to do. An analogy could be drawn with an urban commuter. In deciding whether to drive into town in his own car, or whether to use public transport, it is rational for him to consult his own preferences, and those alone. The fact that if he uses his car he imposes costs on other road users, in terms of delays and higher petrol consumption, is not something that can reasonably be expected to influence his decision — unless, of course, some system of taxes on car-commuting or subsidies to public transport means that the costs to him of the two modes of travel are brought into line with their relative costs to society as a whole.

But while the indifference of governments to the welfare of the inhabitants of other countries may — however regrettable — be understandable, it is less obvious why governments should apparently be uninterested in the effects on their own citizens of the actions that may be taken by foreign governments in response to their own policies. It is true that such effects will often be exceedingly difficult to predict: it is hard enough for a government to predict in detail what will be the effects of its policy decisions on its own target variables; to predict in detail what will be the effects on other countries' target variables, how those countries' governments will react to these effects, and how these reactions will in turn influence the home government's target variables, is something that not even the boldest economic forecaster would claim to be able to do. Nevertheless there is no reason why governments should not make some attempt to think through in broad outline what might be the reactions of other countries to the macroeconomic policies they adopt, and the subsequent repercussions on themselves.

An illustration of what can happen because of governments'

failure to do this is provided by the very restrictive monetary policy adopted in the United States, with little or no consideration of its external effects, in the late 1970s, and its intensification in the early 1980s. One consequence of this policy, and the very high US interest rates it involved, was a marked rise in the value of the dollar against other currencies, notably against the Japanese yen, which fell from around 180 to the dollar in late 1978 to around 280 in late 1982. This meant a very significant increase in the competitiveness of Japanese goods, and a flood of Japanese imports into the United States which had severe effects on output and employment in such bedrock American industries as steel and cars.

Another effect of tight American monetary policies at this time—though one that strays away from the strictly economic field—lay in what happened in the early 1980s to some of the pledges of increased defence expenditure that the United States had elicited from its NATO allies. In West Germany, for example, the deflationary effects of tight monetary policies in the United States, together with the further deflationary effects of the increase in interest rates promoted in Germany in order to prevent an undue fall in the value of the Deutschmark, led, as elsewhere, to a severe recession that reduced the government's tax revenue. Searching for ways to cut public expenditure in order to avoid excessive budget deficits, the government found it politically impossible not to cut back hard on the 3 per cent a year increase in defence expenditure (in real terms) to which it was pledged. In other words, deflationary American monetary policies led directly to a failure to achieve the defence goals which the Americans had set for the Western alliance.

It is, of course, easier to spot consequences of this kind with hindsight than it is to spot them in advance. Nevertheless, it is hard not to believe that there is some scope for incorporating attempts to predict rough feedback effects of this kind into the macroeconomic decision-making process. Up till now, very little effort has been made to do this.

Whatever one's views about the chances of assessing these feedback effects, the more general point seems incontrovertible: there is a strong presumption that economic policy decisions taken by the main OECD countries without much attempt being made to calculate, let alone moderate, the effects on other countries, are likely to result in substantial welfare losses for the world as a whole. The next chapter goes on to consider in more detail the main form that these welfare losses appear to take.

5 The Deflationary Bias

The last chapter pointed out that in an increasingly inter-dependent world, individual countries' economic policies have more effects on other countries than they used to have, yet no account is taken of these effects in framing the policies. The channels through which expansionary or contractionary macroeconomic policies in one country affect key variables in other countries, and perhaps feed back to affect key variables in the first country, were traced in some detail. Although it was pointed out that such myopic decision-taking, like any decision-taking process that ignores important externalities, was likely to result in welfare losses for the world as a whole, nothing was said about the form which such welfare losses do in fact take in the circumstances of the 1980s. This chapter argues that the main form taken by these welfare losses is a loss of output and employment — rather than, for example, a faster rate of inflation or an inefficient allocation of fully-employed resources. There is a deflationary bias in the operation of the international economy, which helps to account for the severe world recession of the early 1980s. Unless the operation of the system is changed, this deflationary bias seems bound to persist, with grave consequences for incomes and employment in the years to come.

Responsibility for this deflationary bias lies in a fundamental asymmetry in the way the international economic system works. The essential nature of this asymmetry can be briefly stated. A country which unilaterally pursues deflationary policies, trying for example to reduce the growth of the money

supply regardless of the implications for output and employment, is likely to be relatively successful in achieving its
deflationary objectives. Moreover it will impose some degree of
deflation not only on itself but also on the other countries with
which it has trading or financial relations; and deflation in
these other countries may feed back into some further degree of
deflation in the original country. A country which unilaterally
pursues an expansionary policy, on the other hand, is much less
likely to do so successfully. Forces at work in the international
economy, which are discussed below, will tend to limit the
extent of any such unilateral expansion, and correspondingly
diminish the degree of stimulus it imparts to other countries.
The net effect of this asymmetry—of the greater staying power
of deflationary than of expansionary policies—is a bias
towards deflation in the world economy as a whole.

The reason for the asymmetry in the working of the
international economic system is fundamentally very simple. It
lies principally in the conflict which exists between the interests
of individual governments on the one hand, and what might be
called the *world financial community* on the other. It is a conflict
very similar to the conflict which a number of observers have
perceived between the interests of the nation-state and the
interests of the multinational corporation;[1] it has echoes, too,
of the conflict between the interests of capital and labour; but it
is somewhat different from both of these.

What is here termed the world financial community finally boils down to a relatively small number of individuals—perhaps only a few hundred—who decide or
advise, on a day-to-day or even hour-to-hour basis, on the
disposition, between different financial assets in different
countries, of funds which collectively run into hundreds of
billions of dollars. The individuals include government and
central bank officials of countries—including particularly
some of the OPEC countries—with large international financial reserves; key figures in the twenty or so largest international private banks; treasurers of multinational corporations—particularly of the giant oil, car and chemical
concerns—and other private sector financial institutions such
as pension funds and insurance companies; and a few particularly influential stockbrokers and financial journalists. The

funds include the foreign exchange reserves of individual countries, the assets and liabilities of international banks and the revenues and working balances of multinational corporations.

As was indicated in Chapter 3, the significance of this world financial community is very much greater than it was ten or fifteen years ago. Eurocurrency deposits—bank deposits denominated in currencies other than that of the (usually European) country in which they are located—hardly existed until the 1960s. Now their gross value is estimated to be $1,500 billion or more. These vast sums, together with huge financial assets held in other forms, such as conventional bank deposits or short-term government securities, are exceedingly mobile: the communications revolution effected by computers and satellites, together with the virtual absence of exchange control in most of the major OECD countries, means that billions of dollars' worth of funds can be switched from one country or currency to another at a moment's notice, twenty-four hours a day, every day of the year.[2] These movements of funds are triggered off by expectations of changes in interest rates, or exchange rates, or rules governing convertibility, or political developments generally. The aim of those charged with the management of these funds is the maximisation of the rate of return earned on them—or, perhaps, the minimisation of risks or losses. They have no interest, as such, in the economic variables which are of concern to governments—the level of unemployment, the rate of growth of the GDP, the inflation rate, or the distribution of income. Their concern is with short-term movements in bond prices, interest rates, exchange rates and so on—the movements likely to take place over the next few weeks or months, often the next few hours. Thus those individuals and institutions which comprise the world financial community have no policy objectives, in the sense in which governments have policy objectives. Governments are trying to *make* things happen to such key economic variables as employment or inflation over a period of two or three years. The world financial community is trying to guess what *will* happen, not primarily to these ultimate economic variables, but to intermediate variables or instruments such as the money supply or interest rates or exchange rates, over a period of a few months at most. The problem with which this chapter is concerned is that in fulfilling this function, the world financial community affects governments' ability to achieve their policy objectives, and does so in an asymmetrical way.

Let us first consider what happens when a country's macroeconomic policies are directed mainly towards reducing the rate of inflation. Unless it places exclusive reliance on an incomes policy, the government will cut back public expenditure and increase taxes in an attempt to reduce the budget deficit, and will take steps to reduce the growth of the money supply. Interest rates will rise, there will be a fall in the level of economic activity, and a corresponding fall in imports, which will strengthen the balance of payments on current account. Higher interest rates, and the prospect of a fall in the inflation rate, will make the country's currency more attractive to the world financial community. There will be an inflow of funds. Under a floating exchange rate regime, this will put upward pressure on the exchange rate. The expectation of a rising exchange rate will prompt a further inflow of funds; and multinational corporations and other traders may reinforce these pressures through the mechanism of leads and lags, speeding up purchases of the home country's currency which they need to make, and delaying sales of it. This will prompt a further rise in the exchange rate, which, by reducing import prices, will enhance the anti-inflationary effects of the country's original policy measures, while at the same time threatening a further twist to the deflationary screw by making its products less competitive in home and export markets. Although this loss of competitiveness will in itself have an encouraging effect on other countries' exports and economic activity, this may be more than offset by the fall in the volume of the home country's imports resulting from its deflationary policies.

If the exchange rate regime is fixed rather than floating, the processes will work somewhat differently. The inflow of capital which represents the world financial community's response to the country's anti-inflationary measures will raise its level of reserves rather than its exchange rate, and unless this rise in reserves is sterilised the home country's actions to reduce the growth of the money supply may be offset to a greater or lesser extent by this inflow of capital. But although in this case the internal impact of the home country's deflationary policies would be reduced, the fact that other countries' currencies had not depreciated against that of the home country, and the contractionary effect on them of an outflow of reserves, would enhance the net deflationary impact on them.

Exactly what will happen in any particular case will depend, of course, not only on whether exchange rates are fixed or floating, but on the numerical values of a whole host of variables and coefficients. But the important point, for present purposes, is this: the response of the world financial community to policies adopted by a country which are expected to reduce its rate of inflation and strengthen its balance of payments and currency is likely, on balance, to *validate* and *reinforce* these policies. The government and its policies receive a vote of confidence from those with the power to move large sums of money in or out of the country. Money will flow in, raising the exchange rate and thus putting further downward pressure on inflation, while at the same time enhancing the deflationary impact on output and employment of the original policy measures.

Things are likely to work very differently in the opposite case, when a government's macroeconomic policies are directed towards increasing the level of output and employment, and raising the rate of growth. In an interdependent world, as was argued in the last chapter, expansionary policies in one country will have expansionary effects on other countries—with possible further repercussions on the original country—*provided that* such expansionary policies are pursued through to fulfilment. The problem is that the responses of the world financial community to such expansionary policies, when adopted by any particular country, are likely to be adverse; and these adverse responses are likely to force the policies to be modified or even abandoned.

An expansionary fiscal policy of a pure kind—i.e. a cut in taxes or increase in public expenditure financed not by increasing the money supply but by selling government bonds to the non-bank private sector—might seem to be the kind of expansionary policy most likely to meet with the approval of the world financial community. This is because it would result in an increase in interest rates, which might be expected to

attract an inflow of capital and thus strengthen the country's
reserves or exchange rate. But the rise in interest rates may be
insufficient to offset the disadvantages of expansion, as seen
through the eyes of the world financial community. These will
include the rise in imports, and hence deteriorating current
account and weakening foreign exchange reserves or exchange
rate, which will be the consequence of expansion undertaken
by one country; and the increased inflationary dangers likely to
stem from the rising pressure of demand in goods markets and
labour markets.

The reaction of the world financial community is likely to be
even less favourable when a fiscal expansion is financed by an
increase in the money supply, or when expansion takes the
form of increasing lending by the banking system to the private
sector. In this case interest rates will tend to fall rather than to
rise, making the country's currency less attractive anyway; and
the basic monetarist assertion that inflation is caused by an
increase in the money supply is by now so deeply embedded in
the subconscious mind of the world financial community that
the threat of a faster-expanding money supply will be a strong
incentive to move financial balances into some other currency.
Depending on whether the exchange rate is fixed or floating,
the expanding country will find that either its reserves or its
exchange rate begin to fall, and this process may accelerate as
more funds are moved out, and traders increasingly hedge
against a fall in the value of the currency by leading and lagging
payments and receipts. The pressures on the government to
modify or even abandon its expansionary policies will mount,
and soon become irresistible. Thus just as contractionary
policies in one country tend to be validated and reinforced by
the responses of the world financial community, expansionary
policies tend to be invalidated and aborted.

But this is not all: there is another factor that has added to
the deflationary bias in the working of the world economy in
recent years. The late 1970s and early 1980s saw the re-
emergence, in all the main OECD countries, of a piece of
dogma which many economists thought had been laid per-
manently to rest by Keynes' *General Theory*. This was the
notion that, regardless of the economic circumstances, a
smaller budget deficit was better than a larger one, and a zero

budget deficit was best of all. The Conservative government elected in Britain in May 1979, for example, soon published a Medium-Term Financial Strategy, according to which the budget deficit (or PSBR) was to fall steadily from about 4 per cent of the GDP to $1\frac{1}{2}$ per cent over a four-year period. In the United States President Reagan, on assuming office in January 1981, promised to balance the Federal budget in 1983–84. In both Germany and Japan, from the late 1970s onward, there was constant agonising about the size of the budget deficit, and constant attempts to reduce it.

The reason for this obsession with budget deficits, at a time when governments were preoccupied with the problem of inflation, is clear enough. In popular mythology (whose influence on practising politicians should not be under-estimated) a government which spends more than it collects in tax revenue finances the difference by 'printing money'—a process which leads to 'too much money chasing too few goods', and accordingly results in inflation. The same chain of events is described in somewhat more sophisticated terms by monetarist economists: unless the budget deficit is financed by borrowing from the non-bank public sector—which would 'crowd out' private investment, with undesirable consequences for re-source allocation and efficiency—it will be financed by borrow-ing from the banking system, and this will lead to an increase in the money supply which in turn will lead to inflation.

There is no doubt that budget deficits *can* be inflationary (though Keynesian economists would argue that the in-flationary mechanism is different from the one posited by the monetarists). But whether they actually are inflationary or, on the contrary, an indicator of the extent of the *deflation* of the economy, will depend on the circumstances of the case. The essence of the matter can be approached in three stages, of steadily increasing complexity.

First, there is the standard Keynesian argument—the fun-damental policy implication of the *General Theory*. If the economy is in a recession, suffering from substantial unem-ployment, one cannot rely on market forces, unaided, to bring the economy back to full employment, at any rate within a reasonable time-scale. Since in these circumstances monetary policy is likely to be ineffective, because however low the rate of interest may be pushed, the probable yield on new investment will be lower, and the risk of undertaking new investment not worthwhile, the government should resort to fiscal policy. By increasing public expenditure, without correspondingly increasing taxation (or, alternatively, reducing taxation without correspondingly cutting public expenditure) the government will 'prime the pump', or inject new purchasing power into the economy. This will lead, by way of the Keynesian multiplier, to successive increases in income and expenditure, and the economy will be brought back to full employment. Initially, of course, this process will involve the government in running a budget deficit. But this is of no particular importance (and in any case may be offset by a budget surplus when full employment has been restored). The government's primary economic responsibility is not to balance its own books, but to ensure that there is a sufficient level of demand in the economy to call forth the desired level of employment. Those who—whether in the 1930s or the 1980s—reject the proposition that the government should run a budget deficit in these recessionary circumstances are relying on the private sector (consumers' expenditure or business investment) or the overseas sector (exports net of imports) to pull the economy out of recession. Neither the experience of the 1930s nor of the early 1980s suggest that this reliance is well-founded.

This leads on to the second stage of the argument. Whether, even at full employment, it is appropriate for a government to balance its budget (or even run a budget surplus) rather than continue to run a budget deficit, is by no means self-evident. It will depend on the relationship, at full employment, between private sector saving and investment, and imports and exports. Assuming, for the sake of simplicity, that exports and imports are equal—i.e. that the balance of payments on current account is in balance—it follows as a matter of arithmetic that the budget surplus or deficit must be matched by an equal private sector deficit or surplus. If—as appears to be the case in most Western countries—private sector saving, at full employment levels of output and income, is greater than private sector investment, there must be a corresponding budget deficit: the excess private sector saving must be lent to the government. Any attempt by the government to resist this process, by balancing—or trying to balance—its budget will exert a deflationary pressure on the economy: output and income will fall until private sector saving and investment are in balance.

The position changes when one relaxes the assumption of current account balance: if exports exceed imports by the same amount that private sector saving exceeds private sector investment, then the government will balance its budget. The private sector will, in effect, be lending its surplus of saving over investment not to the government but to foreigners, so that they may purchase the excess of the home country's exports over its imports.

Thus the appropriate fiscal stance, at full employment levels of income and output, will depend on the relationship between a country's private sector saving and investment and its exports and imports. It will also depend on how far the budget surplus or deficit is regarded as the *cause* of a corresponding private or overseas sector imbalance, and how far the *effect*. Monetarists would tend to argue that a full employment budget deficit (assuming, again, current account balance) is the *cause* of the corresponding private sector surplus: the government borrowing required to finance the budget deficit leads to a rise in interest rates which crowds out private investment, thus reducing it below private saving. It follows from this analysis that a government which runs a budget deficit at full employment is *causing* a misallocation of resources between public and private sectors, or inflation, or both. Keynesians, on the other hand, are more inclined to argue that it is private sector investment and saving which are the causal or exogenous factors, and that if the private sector collectively wants to save more than it wants to invest, the government must respond by running a budget deficit if the economy is not to be set off on a deflationary path.

The appropriate fiscal stance at a time of full employment is not, however, the main issue here. The main issue is the appropriate stance at a time of recession and heavy unemployment, such as that experienced in the early 1980s. And this brings us to the third, and most complicated, aspect of the problem. This lies in the need to distinguish between the influence of the budget on the economy and the influence of the economy on the budget.

One way of looking at this problem is as follows. Suppose that initially the economy is at full employment, and the budget is in balance (with any excess of saving over investment in the private sector being matched by an equal excess of exports over imports). Suppose that there is then a fall in private investment (exports, imports and private saving remaining unchanged) or in exports (private saving, investment and imports remaining unchanged). In either case, arithmetic requires the government's budget to move into deficit. The mechanism of this move into deficit is simple. As private investment or exports fall, output, income and employment will fall. The government will receive less revenue from both direct and indirect taxation, while at the same time it will have to pay out more in the form of social security benefits. The resulting budget deficit will therefore be the *effect* of a *fall* in the level of economic activity. It is a quite different animal from a budget deficit which results from *discretionary* action taken by a government in a recession to increase public expenditure or cut tax rates in order to expand the economy. It is thus a deficit that reflects the influence of the economy on the budget, not one that measures the influence of the budget on the economy.

In order to distinguish between these two very different animals, economists have developed the concept of the 'full employment' or 'cyclically-adjusted' budget balance. This refers to what the budget balance *would* be, given existing tax and social security rates, if the economy were at a full employment level of output, or at any rate at a level of output associated with some particular pressure of demand in the economy, as measured for example by the unemployment rate. In the above example, the *full employment* budget would be in balance even though, because the economy has moved into recession, the *actual* budget is in deficit. If it is assumed that a balanced full employment budget has a neutral effect on the economy,[3] it follows that at a time of recession an actual budget deficit will not be exerting an expansionary or inflationary effect on the economy, as many contemporary politicians and other observers seem to imagine, but a neutral or even deflationary effect. Two examples may serve to illustrate the point. In the United States in 1929—a year of full employment—the actual budget deficit was $1.3 billion. By

1933—at the depth of the depression—the actual budget deficit had risen to $4.7 billion. On the face of it, this would suggest that over the period fiscal policy had become more expansionary. But in fact this rise in the budget deficit was *more* than accounted for by the effects of the depression; on a full employment basis there was a budget *surplus* of $1.7 billion in 1933, indicating that over the period fiscal policy had become more restrictive.[4] A second example relates to recent British experience. In 1980–81 (the first full financial year of the Conservative government elected in May 1979) the actual budget deficit increased significantly, both in absolute terms and as a percentage of GDP. The government responded to this apparently expansionary change by substantially tightening the budget in 1981–82. But the cyclically-adjusted budget deficit had actually *fallen* sharply in 1980–81, indicating that policy had become more restrictive. Thus the tightening of the actual budget in 1981–82 (the reduction in the PSBR) was an inappropriate move. But, because the economy was sliding further into recession, the tightening of the full employment budget was much greater than the tightening of the actual budget.[5] British fiscal policy in 1981–82, in other words, was doubly inappropriate. To respond to a rise in the budget deficit which reflects the falling tax revenues and rising social security benefits resulting from a worsening recession by increases in taxes and cuts in public expenditure designed to reduce the budget deficit is thoroughly perverse. The effect is to drive the economy deeper into recession, and quite possibly to increase the budget deficit even further. It is a gratuitously foolish kind of vicious circle.

Unfortunately this perverse response to the economic difficulties of the last few years has by no means been confined to Britain: it has afflicted most OECD countries. A notable example is Japan. Although Japan invests a relatively high proportion of its GDP, the Japanese propensity to save is even higher.[6] Very little of this excess of private sector saving over private sector investment is invested abroad: even in 1978, when Japan ran a record current account surplus of $18 billion, this represented little more than 2 per cent of the GDP, and the average current account surplus for the five years 1978–82, at about $4 billion, represented little more than a half of one per cent of GDP. The result, *ex post facto*, has been that, as a counterpart to the excess of saving over investment in the private sector, Japan has been running very large budget deficits: during the three years 1978–80, these averaged a little over 10 per cent of GDP.[7] But the Japanese government, far from recognising that it is necessary for the government to borrow on this scale if a large excess of saving over investment in the private sector, in the absence of significant capital exports, is not to lead to a fall in the level of national income, has consistently tried to reduce its budget deficits. The result has been a general deflation of the Japanese economy, with corresponding deflationary effects abroad. As in other countries, concentrating on the actual budget deficit, rather than the full employment or cyclically-adjusted budgetary position, has made things worse: as the Japanese economy has moved away from full employment and full capacity working, the budgetary situation has deteriorated, and measures taken in an attempt to reduce the budget deficit have further worsened the general economic situation.

Thus the failure of OECD governments, at a time of world recession, to look at the cyclically-adjusted budget balance rather than the actual budget balance when formulating macroeconomic policies has had the effect of worsening the recession. There is, to be sure, some excuse for this: it is the *actual* budgetary position that the international financial markets look at. Nor is there much prospect of changing this: the notion that the world financial community might be persuaded to concern itself not with actual budget deficits, but with what the budget deficits would be on a full employment or cyclically-adjusted basis, borders on the fanciful. Nevertheless, the point is so important to rational economic policy-making that governments should make much more effort than they do to emphasise it. But until they do so, it is clear that markets will continue to focus on an entirely inappropriate indicator of what is happening in individual economies. They will look askance not only at budget deficits which result from deliberate expansionary measures adopted by a government, but also at budget deficits which reflect a deepening recession. From their own point of view the first judgment is legitimate, given the divergence of interests between the world financial community and individual governments which was discussed earlier. But the second judgment is illegitimate from any point of view. It is a particularly unfortunate example of the way that individual economies' macroeconomic policies get biased in a deflationary direction.

6 The Deflationary Bias in Operation

In the last chapter it was argued that in the contemporary interdependent world the failure of individual governments to take account of the effects of their macroeconomic policies on other countries has a particular result: a bias towards deflation in the world economy. Whereas deflationary policies adopted by a particular country tend to be validated and reinforced by the responses of the world financial community, expansionary policies are likely to be weakened or reversed. This chapter examines how this mechanism has operated in several of the main OECD countries on a number of occasions over the past decade.

The first significant example worth considering occurred in the wake of the first oil price shock in 1973. It was clear by the beginning of 1974 that the low absorptive capacity of many OPEC countries meant that in the short run only a small proportion of their hugely increased revenues could be spent on imports, and that in 1974, and probably for some years to come, they would be running large current account surpluses. If the level of world economic activity was to be maintained, OECD countries—typically used to being in balance or surplus—would have to accept a large proportion of the counterpart deficit: unwillingness to accept this deficit would inexorably bring into play the only mechanism that could otherwise create an equilibrium between world surpluses and deficits—a fall in the level of world income and output.[1] It is clear that, on an intellectual level, this point was well understood: Finance Ministers of all the main industrial countries issued a statement in January 1974 recognising that for the time being current account deficits had to be accepted, and stressing the importance of sustaining the level of world economic activity.[2] Unfortunately, a number of countries failed entirely to practise what they preached. Germany, temperamentally accustomed to running balance of payments surpluses, and for historical reasons more sensitive to the inflationary effects of the oil price increase than the deflationary implications of the huge potential OPEC surpluses, was the most obvious example. An extremely restrictive budget package had been introduced in May 1973, and little was done during the next two years to mitigate the deflationary effects of this, in spite of the additional deflationary impact of the oil price increase. One consequence of this was that unemployment, which had been about 1 per cent in the middle of 1973, rose to about 5 per cent by the middle of 1975 — in spite of the fact that much of the fall in employment was absorbed not by Germany itself but by the countries of southern Europe which supply Germany with a large number of guestworkers. The deflationary effects on other countries of Germany's economic policy at this time was, however, even greater than these figures would suggest, since its current account surplus, which had been running at an average of less than $2 billion during the years 1970 to 1973, shot up in 1974 to almost $10 billion. This staggering surplus, in a year when the world collectively had to absorb OPEC surpluses of some $60 billion, is an indication of how far German policies were contributing to, rather than mitigating, the deflationary forces at work in the world economy.

Germany was not the only country whose macroeconomic policies at this time were more deflationary than one might have been led to expect by statements about the importance of maintaining world economic activity at a high level and sharing out balance of payments deficits 'fairly'.[3] The same was true of the two biggest OECD economies — the United States and Japan. In the US, monetary policy, which had been growing tighter during 1973, was tightened considerably further in 1974; fiscal policy, too, became increasingly restrictive throughout 1974. Between the second half of 1973 and the first half of 1975 real GDP fell by about 6 per cent. The balance of payments on current account, which had been in deficit during the early 1970s, was roughly in balance in 1974, and then moved into massive surplus—about $12 billion—in 1975. Thus US economic policy, too, compounded rather than alleviated the deflationary effects of the oil price rise. Much the same thing happened in Japan. A contractionary fiscal and monetary policy had been adopted early in 1973, and this was continued throughout 1974 and, in the case of monetary policy, into 1975. This had a dramatic effect on output: industrial production, for example, fell by 20 per cent between late 1973 and early 1975. The effect on Japan's balance of payments of this fall in output, together with an intensified export drive, was equally dramatic. Although the OPEC price increases raised Japan's oil import bill from $6 billion in 1973 to about $20 billion in each of the following three years her current account ran a deficit of less than $5 billion in 1974, was roughly in balance in 1975, and back in substantial surplus by 1976. So Japan's response to the 1973 oil price increase, too, had a deflationary impact both at home and abroad.

There was little or nothing in the workings of the international financial system to deter the US or Germany or Japan from pursuing deflationary policies; they pursued them as long as they wanted, imposing in the process a considerable measure of deflation on other countries in both the developed and developing world. The same cannot be said of other countries which attached more importance to maintaining the level of output and employment in the face of the deflationary impact of the oil price rise, and pursued—or attempted to pursue—reasonably expansionary policies. The logic of the system, and the instincts and calculations of the world financial community, were against them. In Italy, for example, expansion continued quite strongly during the first half of 1974, but then a big outflow of short-term capital, falling foreign exchange reserves and a falling exchange rate forced the imposition of drastic restrictive measures which plunged the country into a deep recession, with falling output and rising unemployment. Much the same happened in France: early in 1974 real GDP seemed set to go on rising at an annual rate of

4–5 per cent well into 1975; but later in the year a slide in the value of the franc, and fears of accelerating inflation, forced the government to introduce a series of austerity measures, with severe consequences for output and employment. In the event GDP, so far from rising by 4 or 5 per cent in 1975, fell by 2 per cent.

It was in Britain, however, that the boldest attempt was made to honour the spirit of the January 1974 Finance Ministers' agreement, and keep the economy expanding even at the cost of a large current account deficit. For some two years after it took office in March 1974 the Labour government pursued fiscal and monetary policies which were mildly expansionary in their effects on demand. Mainly as a result of a rapid rise (in money terms) in public expenditure, the PSBR, as a percentage of the GDP, rose from 6 per cent in 1973–74 to 9 per cent in 1974–75 and $9\frac{1}{2}$ per cent in 1975–76; the Bank of England's minimum lending rate was reduced from 13 per cent to $11\frac{1}{2}$ per cent in the course of 1974, and stayed broadly within a $10–11\frac{1}{2}$ per cent band until the autumn of 1976; and the money supply (as measured by sterling M3) rose fairly steadily, at a rate of 8–10 per cent a year. In consequence, the drop in GDP between the second half of 1973 and the first half of 1975 was only about 1 per cent—much less than the drop in the US and Germany; correspondingly, the rise in unemployment over this period—from about $2\frac{1}{2}$ to $3\frac{1}{2}$ per cent—was also significantly less than in most other countries. Not surprisingly, however, one result of Britain's attempt to go on expanding while other countries contracted was a large balance of payments deficit—considerably larger than would have been its counterpart 'fair share' of the OPEC surpluses. In 1974 it ran a current account deficit of about $\$8\frac{1}{2}$ billion—bigger than that of any other country; and in 1975 it had a deficit of about $4 billion—bigger than any other country except Canada. It was still running a deficit, at an annual rate of about $2 billion, during the first half of 1976. These deficits would of course have been smaller if other countries had also been following expansionary policies, and thus importing more from Britain. But they were not. In the circumstances the deficits, however much they might reflect a praiseworthy attempt to pursue policies that were rational from the point of view of the world as a whole, were bound to become a matter of increasing concern both at home and abroad.

There was another aspect of Britain's economic performance in 1974–75 which caused increasing concern, not least to the world financial community: a rising inflation rate. This was not the consequence of a high or rising pressure of demand in the economy—as was indicated above, unemployment was increasing during this period, albeit relatively slowly—and thus cannot be attributed to the mildly expansionary posture of the government's economic policies. It was, rather, the result of two other factors. One of these was the system of 'threshold agreements', a feature of the incomes policy introduced earlier by the Heath government which was designed to secure trade union acceptance of low wage increases by promising that if prices rose faster than expected, wages would be allowed to rise in order to compensate. Because the strength of the 1972–73 commodity price boom had been underestimated in Whitehall, and the oil price increase not foreseen at all, retail prices in Britain were 11 per cent higher in October 1974 than had been forecast a year earlier. As a result, the wages of most workers had been automatically raised by approximately an extra 11 per cent as well (over and above the 7 or 8 per cent increase negotiated under the terms of the incomes policy) and this inevitably fed through into further price increases.

Even more important than this, however, was another factor: the political circumstances surrounding the fall of the Heath government early in 1974. During the election campaign the Opposition Labour party in effect promised the country's striking miners that if elected it would pay them the 30 per cent wage increase they were demanding. It was elected, and honoured its somewhat dishonourable pledge. But because of the importance of traditional differentials and relativities in British collective bargaining, the fact that the miners had got a 30 per cent increase meant that before long a great many other groups of workers had demanded—and often obtained—an increase of around 30 per cent as well. These huge wage increases were soon passed on in higher prices, and by mid-1975 the year-on-year inflation rate, at 26 per cent, was beginning to assume Latin American proportions. Meanwhile, the exchange rate had started to fall. The pound had been worth $2–42 in March 1975; by July it had fallen by 10 per cent, to $2–19. The government sensed that the psychological moment had come to introduce the incomes policy which, as a party in Opposition, it had sworn to avoid, but which some of its more realistic members had always known would be necessary. An agreement was hastily reached with the trade unions under which, during the twelve months to August 1976, no one should receive a wage increase of more than £6 a week, or approximately 10 per cent.

This incomes policy proved remarkably effective: weekly earnings, which had risen by nearly 30 per cent between mid-1974 and mid-1975, rose by only about 15 per cent over the next twelve months and—under the second phase of the incomes policy, agreed between the government and the unions in the spring of 1976—by only 10 per cent between mid-1976 and mid-1977. (By the time the government left office in May 1979 the inflation rate had been brought down to below 10 per cent.) Ironically, however, it was only in the early spring of 1976, after it had become clear that the incomes policy was working, and after there had been a considerable improvement in the balance of payments compared to the position in 1974, that the real loss of confidence in Britain's economic policies began. This was partly occasioned by the undoubted fact that public expenditure had been rising very rapidly, largely in order to finance the huge public sector pay increases of 1974–75, though also because the government had attempted to moderate the rise in retail prices—and hence, under the 1973–74 'threshold agreements', the rise in wages—by increasing subsidies to such sectors as food, transport and housing. In consequence, public expenditure as a proportion of the GDP shot up from $40\frac{1}{2}$ per cent in 1973–74 to $45\frac{1}{2}$ per cent in 1974–75, a proportion which remained much the same in 1975–76.[4] Nearly half of this increase was in fact financed out of the buoyancy of the revenue—i.e. out of the higher tax revenue accruing from the higher level of income and expenditure—and the rest was financed without recourse to borrowing from the banking system. Thus even in monetarist eyes the budget deficit (as opposed to the big rise in public sector wages underlying it, which was now being brought under control by the incomes policy) could not really be inflationary. Moreover in February 1976 the government announced that the public expenditure planned for 1977–78 and beyond would be cut back. Nevertheless, predictably, financial opinion in the City of London took an unfavourable view of the rise in public expenditure, and communicated its view to financial opinion abroad. Another factor behind the loss of confidence in the early spring of 1976 was the belief that gained ground that the Treasury and Bank of England were trying to engineer a further fall in the exchange rate.[5] Even though the dollar rate had fallen to about $2–00 by early March (compared with a rate of about $2–40 a year earlier), the government was rumoured to take the view that this fall was insufficient to offset the loss of competitiveness resulting from Britain's recent high inflation rate. If the British government thought sterling was too high, no one else was going to buy it and a lot of people were going to sell it. Thus the rate started to slide, and by early June had fallen by 15 per cent, to $1–70. Afraid that the fall might get completely out of hand, the government hastily negotiated a $5.3 billion swap arrangement with the US and European central banks. At the insistence of the US Treasury and Federal Reserve Board, however, both of which were at this time under the control of hard-liners, this $5.3 billion was made available for only six months, and it was made clear that in no circumstances would it be renewed. In effect this meant that if any of the money was used, Britain would need to negotiate a loan from the IMF—with all the conditions always attached to such loans—by early December.

For the rest of the year Britain wriggled desperately in an effort to get off this hook. In July a deflationary package of payroll tax increases and further public expenditure cuts for 1977–78, amounting altogether to some £2 billion—about $1\frac{1}{2}$ per cent of the GDP—was announced. Early in September, after more than a quarter of the $5.3 billion had been used up in supporting sterling, the Bank of England's minimum lending rate was raised from $11\frac{1}{2}$ per cent to 13 per cent. Late in September the Chancellor of the Exchequer had to abandon—as he was about to board the plane at Heathrow airport—his journey to the annual meeting of the IMF because of a further sharp drop in the pound. Early in October MLR was raised again, to 15 per cent. The Prime Minister, Mr Callaghan, tried hard to get the Americans and Germans to provide a 'safety net' for the official sterling balances, so that overseas governments which still held their reserves in the form of sterling could withdraw their funds from London without precipitating a sterling crisis. It was no good. The world financial community, and not least its archetypal representatives at the US Treasury,[6] had simply decided that the Labour government in Britain was thoroughly profligate, that public expenditure and the PSBR were out of control, and that the nation was heading for bankruptcy. By late October confidence had so eroded that the dollar exchange rate was down to $1–56, a fall of almost a quarter since the beginning of the year. If a vicious interaction of a plunging exchange rate and an accelerating inflation rate was to be avoided, international financial opinion had to be propitiated; and this could only be done by calling in the IMF. The IMF was duly called in and, as it usually does, prescribed a stiff dose of deflationary medicine: public expenditure must be cut by £3 billion (6 per cent) in 1977–78 and £4 billion (8 per cent) in 1978–79; the PSBR must be cut from an estimated 9 per cent of the GDP in 1976–77 to 6 per cent in 1977–78 and 5 per cent in 1978–79; and the growth of the money supply must be reined back.[7]

The crunch came at a series of Cabinet meetings early in December, at which a group of ministers led by the Foreign Secretary, Anthony Crosland, argued against the kind of deflationary policies being demanded by the IMF. With unemployment at 1.3 million (about $5\frac{1}{2}$ per cent) and moving upwards, said Crosland, there was plenty of spare capacity in the economy, and no need for a further round of public expenditure cuts in addition to those already agreed on two separate occasions earlier in the year. Such cuts might in any case be counterproductive, since they might alienate the trade unions and jeopardise the voluntary but crucially important incomes policy, now half way through its second year. Nor would such cuts necessarily have much effect in reducing the PSBR—the size of which so exercised financial opinion—since by creating more unemployment they would increase social security payments and depress tax revenue. Thus there was no objective case for accepting the IMF's proposals. Crosland conceded that something might need to be done to cope with the subjective, or 'confidence' factor, and proposed a system of import deposits, of the kind that had been briefly used by the last Labour government in the late 1960s. By requiring importers to deposit a proportion of the value of their imports with the government for six months or so, this scheme would both restrain imports and thus improve the balance of payments, and help to finance the PSBR. However, Crosland's solution was not supported by either the Prime Minister or the Chancellor of the Exchequer, and the IMF's terms for a loan were accepted—though at least by now the demand for cuts in public expenditure of £3 billion in 1977–78 and £4 billion in 1978–79 had been whittled down to £$1\frac{1}{2}$ billion and £2–$2\frac{1}{2}$ billion respectively.

For the next two years or so British economic policy was constrained by the need to comply with the IMF conditions. Ironically, these constraints turned out to be largely academic. A tough new system of cash limits designed to enforce the public expenditure cuts the government had decided on long before the IMF had appeared on the scene proved, if anything, too effective, leading to big shortfalls in planned expenditure. In the financial year 1976–77 (two-thirds of which had already elapsed by the time the IMF agreement had been signed) the volume of public expenditure turned out to have been $3\frac{1}{2}$ per cent *lower* than in 1975–76.[8] In 1977–78 (the first financial year covered by the IMF conditions) public expenditure was 6–7 per cent *below* the level demanded by the IMF. Correspondingly, it turned out that the PSBR, about which so much fuss had been made, had already fallen from $9\frac{1}{2}$ per cent of the GDP in 1975–76 to $6\frac{1}{2}$ per cent in 1976–77—at the time of the IMF agreement, in December 1976, it had been estimated to be 9 per cent in 1976–77—and it fell to less than 4 per cent in 1977–78—compared with the 6 per cent demanded by the IMF.

However all this is, in a sense, irrelevant to what happened in 1976, since it was only considerably later that the magnitude of the squeeze on public expenditure that was already taking place came to be appreciated. What happened in 1976 was that a major industrial country was forced, because of the disapproval of its mildly social democratic and expansionary policies felt by the world financial community and a business-oriented regime in Washington, to apply to the IMF for a loan, and to accept terms for the loan that seemed at the time to be very close to national humiliation. Whether this outcome could have been avoided by adopting Crosland's proposals will never be known. Judging by the experience of the late 1960s, an import deposits scheme would not have had much effect on the volume of imports, though it could have made quite a sizeable contribution to financing the PSBR by means of the forced loans made by importers or their overseas suppliers to the government. But it seems doubtful whether this would have done the trick: the US Administration, and the world financial community generally, had taken the view that only surveillance by the IMF would bring the British government back to responsible economic policies, and nothing short of that would now do.

The only alternative to bowing to the demands of American and world financial opinion would have been to adopt policies which did not require their approval. Such a course was indeed recommended to the Cabinet by the leading left-winger Tony Benn, who called for the imposition of drastic import and exchange controls, the extensive direction of investment by the state, and other measures appropriate to a wartime siege economy. Whatever the merits of such a system as a long-term objective (and they are discussed in the next chapter), as a solution to the crisis of late 1976 it was wholly unrealistic. Long before the apparatus of such a siege economy could have been constructed—indeed probably within hours of a decision to construct it becoming known—money would have been pouring out of the country, the pound would be threatening to sink out of sight, and the financial markets would be in a state of chaos. The Labour government—by now in a minority in the House of Commons—would almost certainly have fallen.

That Britain—long considered something of an economic cripple by hard-line world financial opinion—should be forced by international pressures to adopt deflationary policies that were highly unwelcome to its government may not seem altogether surprising. But a couple of years later something very similar happened to the United States. This was much more surprising. The US, after all, still had far and away the world's biggest economy, with a GDP three times as big as Japan's and four times as big as Germany's; and for most of the post-war era its currency had been the foundation of the international monetary system.

The US economy recovered strongly from the recession of 1974–75, and during 1976, 1977 and 1978, helped a little by the moderately expansionary measures adopted by the Carter Administration, which took office in January 1977, the GDP grew at a steady rate of about 5 per cent a year. This was not an excessive rate of growth by American standards, though there was some fall in unemployment over these three years, from about $7\frac{1}{2}$ per cent to $5\frac{1}{2}$ per cent of the labour force, and a slight rise in the inflation rate, from about $7\frac{1}{2}$ per cent to 9 per cent. The significant fact, however, was that the US was unique in expanding at this sort of rate during this period: the rest of OECD was pursuing more cautious policies, and only growing at two-thirds of the US rate. The result should have come as no surprise: a worsening US balance of payments and a currency coming under increasing pressure. The American current account surplus of $12 billion in 1975 was eliminated in 1976 and became a deficit of $17 billion in 1977—a figure which hardly improved in 1978. Against the other major world currencies the dollar began to fall, and went on falling. Measures were taken in the early autumn of 1978 that were reminiscent of the measures taken in Britain a couple of years earlier: the Federal Reserve Board raised its discount rate to the unprecedented level of $8\frac{1}{2}$ per cent, and the President announced a deflationary package, including public expenditure cuts, a reduction in the Budget deficit, and the introduction of a voluntary prices and incomes policy. It was no good: the dollar continued to fall. By the end of October 1978 it had depreciated, compared with two years earlier, by some 20 per cent against sterling, 30 per cent against the Deutschmark, and 40 per cent against the Swiss franc and Japanese yen. The rot was only stopped at the beginning of November, when the Administration announced that it had negotiated a package which would provide $30 billion worth of foreign exchange to support the dollar in the foreign exchange markets. Half of this would be provided by swap arrangements with the central banks of Germany, Japan and Switzerland, and another $10 billion by the issuing of US government securities denominated in foreign currencies. $3 billion of the rest was financed by borrowing from the IMF, though as this was under the reserve tranche provision, it did not make the US subject to the kind of conditionality imposed two years earlier on Britain.

The President's deflationary measures, together with the package of foreign exchange support, were successful in the sense that they halted the decline of the dollar. After a slight recovery it stabilised, and—helped on occasion by massive intervention—its effective value (in terms of a basket of other currencies) showed little change for the next two years. There was, however, a price to be paid: during the same two years (1979 and 1980) GDP grew by less than 1 per cent a year, and unemployment rose from $5\frac{1}{2}$ per cent back to $7\frac{1}{2}$ per cent. In short, what had happened earlier to France, Italy and Britain had now happened to the United States: expansionary policies undertaken when other major countries were not expanding had aroused the distrust of the world financial community, which had voted by moving out its money; and eventually the expansion had had to be abandoned.

The trauma of the dollar was not completely ended by the package announced in November 1978. The currency came under pressure again in the summer of 1979, as world financial opinion—to some extent influenced by the election of a hard-line monetarist government in Britain—increasingly took the view that the American money supply was being allowed to rise too fast, and that inflationary forces were gathering momentum. There was substantial intervention in the foreign exchange markets in support of the dollar; the Federal Reserve discount rate was raised in stages from $9\frac{1}{2}$ per cent in July to a record 12 per cent in early October; and—perhaps most significantly of all—it was announced early in October that henceforth the Federal Reserve Board would concentrate on controlling the monetary base—the reserves held by the commercial banks at the Federal Reserve—rather than interest rates. The implication was that the growth of the money supply would now be controlled more directly and more consistently, regardless of the effect on interest rates.

October 1979 can be seen as marking the point at which US economic policies ceased being determined—as they had been for the past year—by restrictive actions and attitudes else-where, and instead became the determinant of deflationary policies in other countries. The United States stopped being a victim, and started being an aggressor. This process became much more pronounced after the election of President Reagan in November 1980. The Reagan Administration's economic philosophy was very similar to that of the Thatcher govern-ment which had taken office eighteen months earlier in Britain. Inflation was seen as the main enemy, and was to be brought down to a low figure by a combination of cuts in public expenditure, (except on defence, where expenditure was to rise), a reduction in the budget deficit, and tight control of the money supply. At the same time direct taxes were to be cut—the famous 'supply side' measures—in order to unleash entrepreneurial energies and increase the incentive to innovate, to invest and to save. The result of this would be a faster-growing economy, so that even though tax *rates* were lower, total tax *revenue* would be higher.

Alas, the supply-side scenario turned out—as its critics had always predicted—to be a fairy story; something smacking more of Disneyland than Washington. President Reagan found, as Mrs Thatcher had found, that the supply-side tax cuts—mainly of benefit to the very wealthy—had no effect whatever in unleashing energies or increasing investment and saving: all they did was to make the rich richer and reduce total tax revenue. The President also discovered, as had Mrs Thatcher, that it was much easier to increase expenditure on defence than it was to cut public expenditure of other kinds. The result of this double *débâcle* was that the budget deficit did not fall, but rose. The actual budget deficit for the fiscal year during which President Reagan took office—1980–81, ending on 30 September 1981—turned out to be $58 billion. He proposed to reduce the deficit to $45 billion in 1981–82, and to eliminate it altogether by 1983–84. In fact the deficit in 1981–82 turned out to be over $100 billion, and in 1982–83 looked like being around $200 billion, or 6 per cent of GNP. Nothing more was heard about balancing the budget in 1983–84.

The combination of a high and prospectively rising budget deficit and a money supply tightly controlled by the independent Federal Reserve Board led to very high rates of interest. That there should have been some increase in interest rates in this situation is understandable: as was pointed out in Chapter 4, if a budget deficit has to be financed by bond sales, because policy is to prevent the money supply being expanded beyond certain rigid limits, there will inevitably be some downward pressure exerted on the price of bonds, and hence some upward pressure on interest rates. But the increase in interest rates which actually occurred in the United States at this time was very big. Between the beginning of 1981 and the middle of 1982, for example, the rate on 3-month money market instruments averaged over 15 per cent—a figure two or three times as high as in the mid-1970s, and implying actual bank lending rates to industrial and personal borrowers which often approached 20 per cent. Whether interest rates as high as this were inevitable—an inescapable consequence of the way the economic system works—is debatable. It is often argued that, whatever the government's intentions, big budget deficits inevitably lead to big increases in the money supply, which inevitably lead to a rise in the inflation rate, and that high money rates of interest merely reflect the anticipation of this higher inflation rate. This argument is not very convincing: the links between budget deficits and the money supply, and the money supply and the inflation rate, are much too tenuous and unpredictable to justify the claim that very high US interest rates in 1981 and 1982 were unavoidable, given the size of prospective budget deficits. It might, indeed, make more sense to reverse the causal sequence, and argue that, because of the heavy weight of debt interest in Federal government expenditure, budget deficits were expected to be high in large part because interest rates were expected to be high; in other words that high interest rates made big budget deficits unavoidable, and not the other way round.

Whatever one's views on these questions, it is clear that by early 1981 monetarist ways of looking at the economy had acquired such a grip on Wall Street and other financial markets that large American budget deficits were *expected* to lead to high interest rates; and, such is the power of expectations in financial markets, they duly did so. Prime rates of interest—the rates charged by the commercial banks to their most creditworthy customers—which had temporarily been as low as 11 per cent in August 1980, shot up to over 20 per cent at the beginning of 1981, and for the next year and a half fluctuated in roughly the 15–20 per cent range. Given that the annual inflation rate was below 10 per cent during most of 1981, and fell considerably further in 1982, this implied that for much of the time real interest rates were running at an unprecedented 10 per cent or more. It is hardly surprising that industries heavily dependent on credit sales, such as housing and cars, should have been decimated, or that the American economy as a whole should have been plunged into deep recession. Between the middle of 1981 and the end of 1982 US industrial production fell by 10 per cent, and unemployment rose from $7\frac{1}{2}$ per cent to 10 per cent.

These American policies, and in particular the very high rates of interest which they involved, had a devastating effect on the entire world economy—an effect which the US Administration either did not notice or did not mind. There used to be a saying that when America sneezed, the rest of the world caught a cold. What people had in mind was the effect of a recession in the huge American economy on its imports—and therefore other countries' exports—and on the world prices of the primary commodities of which the US is such a major consumer. This traditional impact has certainly made itself felt over the last few years, but has been outweighed in importance by the consequences of the much greater degree of *financial* interdependence in the world economy than obtained twenty years ago: it is capital flows, rather than trade flows, which have caused the real trouble. Very high American interest rates meant a massive influx of capital into the United States and dollar-denominated financial assets. Other developed countries were faced with the choice of trying to hold down their own interest rates and seeing a marked depreciation of their currency in terms of the dollar, or of trying to maintain parity with the dollar and accepting a big rise in their domestic interest rates. The first course threatened—because so many world prices, including the price of oil, are fixed in terms of dollars—to raise import prices and increase the inflation rate; the second threatened deepening domestic recession and rising unemployment. Countries varied in their response, but the overall effect was a good deal of each. The effective exchange rate of the dollar against other currencies rose—in the complete absence of intervention in the foreign exchange markets by the Reagan Administration—by no less than 30 per cent between late 1980 and the middle of 1982; at the same time interest rates in most developed countries rose to historically unprecedented levels, with correspondingly adverse effects on output and employment. Industrial production in OECD countries was flat from 1979 onwards, and GDP only increased by about 1 per cent a year. Because of the system of lifetime employment, open unemployment in Japan showed little rise; but in the countries of the EEC it rose from around 5 per cent in mid-1979 to 10 per cent by the end of 1982. Many developing and Eastern bloc countries suffered doubly—not only from the effect on the volume and price of their exports of the marked slowing down of growth in the developed countries, but also from the higher interest rates they now had to pay on their external debt.

The devastating side-effects of American policies pursued for almost exclusively domestic reasons can be illustrated by reference to West Germany. If there was any single OECD country which might have been thought relatively immune to the direct and indirect effects of high American interest rates it was Germany, a country with a prodigious record of low inflation, balance of payments surpluses and a rock-hard currency. But not even Germany is exempt from the deflationary bias inherent in the operation of the international financial markets. In 1978, under pressure from other OECD countries to reduce its persistent balance of payments surpluses and speed up its relatively sluggish rate of growth, Germany had reluctantly taken expansionary measures on essentially 'altruistic' grounds—measures it would not have taken had it been concerned with the immediate welfare of its own citizens alone. Unfortunately for the prospects for future international economic co-operation of this kind, these expansionary measures turned out to be something of a mistake from the strictly German point of view. Under the stimulus of faster expansion the 1978 balance of payments surplus of $9 billion was turned into a $5 billion deficit in 1979, and in 1980, as a consequence also of the 1979–80 oil price increase, rose to $16 billion. The

Deutschmark remained remarkably steady against the dollar, at a rate of around 1–80, until late 1980, when it started to move down. The traditional German fear of the faster inflation that would follow a depreciating currency, together with the need to attract capital inflows to finance the large current account deficit, prompted the Bundesbank to raise interest rates to record levels early in 1981. All that this seems to have done is to have moderated the decline in the Dm against the dollar, which moved from about Dm 1–90 at the end of 1980 to Dm 2–25 at the end of 1981, and to around Dm 2–60 by late 1982. Nevertheless, these very high domestic interest rates—which, because of the low German inflation rate, were very high in real and not just in nominal terms—together with the restrictive fiscal policies the German government felt it necessary to pursue for a mixture of anti-inflation and confidence reasons, combined to halt the German economy in its tracks. GDP, which grew by less than 2 per cent in 1980, fell in 1981, and fell further in 1982. Investment also fell. Unemployment, which had been about 3 per cent early in 1980, had risen to 7 per cent by the end of 1982, and showed every sign of going on rising. This sharp rise in unemployment did not merely cause widespread concern in Germany: it directly threatened the continued existence of the coalition government (which did in fact fall late in 1982, though not for exclusively economic reasons). Yet the fear of what might happen to the dollar value of the Deutschmark if there were any significant reduction in interest rates inhibited effective action. The German government was reduced to criticising high American interest rates and the Administration's refusal to intervene at all in the foreign exchange markets: an impotent spectator of events over which it regarded itself as having no control.

Thus the deflationary bias inherent in the attitudes and operations of the world financial community made itself felt even in Germany. But of course the deflationary effect of high American interest rates were by no means confined to Germany among European countries. Apart from direct effects, the commitment of countries belonging to the European Monetary System to maintain their mutual exchange rates within narrow limits meant that high interest rates in Germany were bound to lead to high interest rates in other member countries as well. This in turn had deflationary effects in these countries, and this in turn, via the dampening effects on their imports, contributed further to the deflation of the world economy as a whole.

Even Japan, the most dynamic of all the OECD economies, found its policies severely constrained by high American interest rates. Japan had recovered so well from the first oil shock that by 1978 it was running a huge current account surplus of some $17 billion. Pressed, like Germany, to adopt expansionary measures—and special steps to liberalise imports—it responded sufficiently to keep GDP rising at a rate of about 5 per cent a year. Partly because of this but mainly as a result of the second oil price increase, the balance of payments ran quite large deficits in 1979 and 1980. These deficits, together with the effects on capital account of the rising trend of US interest rates and the lifting of restrictions on foreign investment by Japanese residents, put downward pressure on the yen, which fell by about 20 per cent, in dollar terms, between early 1979 and early 1980. In response to this, interest rates were raised in 1980 to record levels, and there was a sharp recovery in the value of the yen. For the next two years, however, Japan hovered between the horns of a dilemma. If it kept interest rates very high it would cripple the domestic economy—especially since the very low Japanese inflation rate meant that nominal interest rates high enough to discourage a capital outflow to the US would imply very high real rates of interest.[9] If, on the other hand, it reduced interest rates in line with domestic requirements, there would be an outflow of capital which would cause a further fall in the already undervalued yen. This would not only pose some inflationary threat, but would also increase the danger of US and European protectionist measures against the rising tide of Japanese exports which would follow.

In the event, the Japanese government plumped for some of each. There were some reductions in interest rates from late 1980 onwards, and the yen slid down against the dollar until, in late 1982, it reached a five-year low of around 280 to the dollar. Although the depreciation against other currencies was much smaller—indeed the yen appreciated against the Deutschmark over this period—the overall effect was likely to be rising

Japanese exports and the re-emergence of unacceptably large current account surpluses, leading to intense pressure on Japan to restrict its exports and increase its imports. Nevertheless, the fall in interest rates and relaxation of credit controls were not large enough to meet the demands of the domestic economy: growth slowed markedly in 1981, and the GDP actually fell in the last quarter of that year. Growth continued to be slow in 1982.

The deflationary policies forced on the United States by the world financial community late in 1978, and voluntarily intensified by the Reagan Administration after the beginning of 1981 were, in their own terms, successful. The balance of payments on current account moved from deficit into surplus, the dollar strengthened enormously, and the inflation rate was eventually brought down to below 5 per cent. The price, however, was heavy: stagnant or falling output not only in the US, but in much of the rest of the world as well.

By mid-1982, nothing had happened to deflect the US Administration from its deflationary course: its policies continued to receive the support of the world financial community. But by this time there was another example of the other kind—the stifling of expansionary initiatives by the workings of the international financial system: the experience of France in 1981–82. In the Presidential election held in May 1981, against a background of stagnant GDP, falling industrial production and rapidly rising unemployment—all of them, in part at any rate, the consequence of American policies since 1979—the incumbent President Giscard d'Estaing was defeated by the Socialist candidate Francois Mitterrand. Whereas Giscard's priorities had been lower inflation and a strong exchange rate, Mitterrand—whose position was soon strengthened by the election of a National Assembly with a strong left-wing majority—took office pledged to expand the economy by a combination of conventional Keynesian policies and greater central direction of industry. In order to expand effective demand, low wages and many social security payments were to be increased; and although part of the consequent increase in public expenditure would be financed by higher taxes on the wealthy and windfall taxes on banks and oil companies, it was accepted that for a while there would be larger budget deficits. At the same time, the economy's deeper structural problems were to be tackled by an ambitious programme of research, training and investment in new technologies, co-ordinated and financially assisted by the state, which would extend its ownership and control of the manufacturing and banking sectors.

The world financial community—including that part of it resident in France—did not like the sound of this at all. It was not interested in the beneficial effects the programme might have on employment and real incomes in France, particularly in the longer run. Its concern was with the effects on inflation and the value of the franc in the short run. These, it assumed—making what was to some extent a self-fulfilling prophecy—would be unfavourable. Thus Mitterrand's election was followed by a substantial run on the franc, which was only stemmed when short-term interest rates were raised to 20 per cent or more. But this alleviation could only be temporary. There was no way, in an open trading system, in which France could pursue expansionary policies while other major countries were pursuing deflationary policies, without running into balance of payments problems. Similarly there was no way, even though it had a fairly sophisticated apparatus of exchange controls, in which France could pursue policies deemed by the financial markets to be inflationary and socialistic without the franc coming under heavy pressure. Either it would have to use up its foreign exchange reserves defending the franc—as indeed it was required to do, up to a point, as long as it remained a member of the European Monetary System—or it would have to devalue, thus risking a further boost to inflation, which would itself put further downward pressure on the currency. Although the government tried to accommodate these forces without abandoning its expansionary plans, devaluing the franc by 3 per cent in the EMS in October 1981, introducing a partial price freeze, and starting discussions with the unions about an incomes policy, there was no escaping the logic of the situation. As the outlook for inflation and the balance of payments worsened, businesses in France cut back their investment plans, capital moved out, and the franc came under renewed pressure. In the early summer of 1982—barely a year after Mitterrand's election—the government gave up the struggle. An austerity package was introduced, comprising not only a further devaluation of the franc and a wage and price freeze, but cuts in public expenditure designed to effect a significant reduction in the budget deficit. Even tougher austerity measures had to be introduced early in 1983. The result, it was acknowledged, would be stagnant or falling output and rising unemployment. The deflationary bias in the working of the international economic system had claimed another victim.

*

This chapter has been concerned with the deflationary bias attending national economic decision-making in an inter-dependent world. When a particular country adopts policies which have the effect of depressing output and employment, the deflationary impact of these policies is likely to be passed on to other countries — particularly when the deflating country is the United States, which still accounts for some 40 per cent of the GDP of the total OECD area. When a country adopts expansionary policies, on the other hand — even if it is the United States — the result is less likely to be the transmission of expansionary effects to other countries than the discourage-ment of these expansionary policies by the conditioned reflexes of the world financial community. To be sure, there are some exceptions to this rule. The large US current account deficits in 1977 and 1978 which resulted from that country's expan-sionary policies in 1976–78, for example, led to a very big inflow of dollars into West Germany and Switzerland — not just to finance the US deficits, but as a natural response of the world financial community to the fact that during this period the US was expanding considerably faster than anybody else. Under the rules of the floating exchange rate game, this inflow of capital would normally have led to a rise in the value of the Deutschmark and Swiss franc, so that the expansionary effects on the German and Swiss economies of the dollar inflow would have been minimised. Up to a point this did happen, but the German and Swiss governments became alarmed at the extent to which the appreciation of their currencies was pricing their producers out of export markets, and intervened to hold down the extent of the appreciation. The consequence was a substantial increase in the money supply in both countries, and a general expansionary impetus to their domestic economies—though the effect on inflation was much smaller than monetarist theories would have predicted.

This, however, was a fairly rare exception. The more general rule over the past decade has been that expansionary policies pursued by an individual country have had to be abandoned, because of the reactions of the international markets, before they have had much chance to exert an expansionary influence on other countries. This was true of Britain, France and Italy in 1974–76, of France in 1981–82, and indeed, after a while, of the United States in 1976–78. On the other hand deflationary policies in one country led to deflationary consequences in others—not just through the traditional trade channels, but through the operations of the international financial markets, reflecting the instincts and calculations of the world financial community. And deflationary consequences in these other countries led back in turn to further deflationary effects in the original country. The net result was that everyone ended up with lower output and higher unemployment than anyone had intended.

7 De-link, or Co-ordinate?

The last two chapters have provided reasons for supposing that there is a deflationary bias in the working of the international economy, arising primarily from the fact that the world financial community tends to validate deflationary policies and discourage expansionary ones. The consequences of this deflationary bias were at their most acute in 1982, when unemployment in OECD countries was at levels unprecedented since the great slump in the 1930s, and still rising. Deflationary policies had been successfully pursued in a number of countries, most notably in the United States and Britain, and had spread deflation to the rest of the world. Attempts at expansion, most notably in France, had got nowhere.

Viewed even from the standpoint of those governments, like the Reagan Administration in the US and the Thatcher government in Britain, which saw themselves as having a mandate to bring down the inflation rate even if this involved heavy unemployment, this state of affairs was unsatisfactory: unemployment was much higher than had been anticipated a couple of years earlier, in large part because neither government had made allowance for the deflationary effects their policies would have on other countries, or how these deflationary effects would in turn feed back to them. Viewed from the standpoint of governments, such as the Mitterrand

Administration in France, the SPD-FDP coalition in Germany, and a number of other OECD governments, which were constrained from pursuing what they considered desirable growth and employment policies by the deflationary working of the international monetary system, the situation was less satisfactory still. If they are to escape from this deflationary trap, there are logically only two strategies which such countries can pursue or promote. One is to withdraw in some degree from the international economic community, reversing the increased interdependence of the last decade or two by reducing the trading and financial links which make the attainment of a country's economic objectives so dependent on events and decisions elsewhere. The other is to seek to achieve a much greater degree of international co-ordination of national economic policies, so that the effects on other countries of national policy decisions are assessed as fully as possible when the decisions are made, and thus the deflationary bias in the working of the international economy taken explicitly into account and allowed for when policies are formulated. The advantages and disadvantages of each of these strategies will be considered in turn.

The first strategy—what might be called *de-linking* to some extent from the international economy—would have two main ingredients: import controls and exchange controls. Import controls would ensure that an expansion of effective demand engineered by fiscal and monetary policies would be met predominantly by domestic output, thus leading to a reduction in unemployment at home, rather than by an increase in the level of imports, which worsened the balance of payments and mainly reduced unemployment abroad. Exchange controls would ensure that the country's residents—and perhaps to some extent non-residents as well—would only obtain foreign exchange in return for the country's own currency for purposes approved by the government. This would help to reduce the economy's vulnerability to adverse developments in the outside world, partly because it could be decreed that a fall in export earnings would lead to cuts only in less essential imports, foreign exchange continuing to be allocated for purchases of essential materials and equipment. More importantly, however, it would reduce the country's vulnerability to

any unfavourable judgments of its policies formed by the
international money markets. The restrictions imposed by the
government on the official convertibility of its currency—i.e.
on outward capital flows—would limit the extent of the
pressures on its exchange rate or foreign exchange reserves
resulting from the deflationary bias of the instincts and
attitudes of the world financial community.

Making in the first instance the simplifying assumptions that
such controls are imposed by one country alone, that they are
effective in their operation, and that there is no retaliation by
other countries, then the advantages to the country in question
are likely to be substantial. It would be able to expand output
and employment at the rate permitted by the supply-side
factors in its own economy. Obviously, the more flexible and
adaptable the economy, and the greater the ease with which
capital and labour flow out of old industries and occupations
and into new ones, the faster the rate of expansion can be.
Obviously, too, the government in its decisions will trade off a
faster rate of expansion against a faster rate of inflation: an
increase in effective demand that is not permitted to be satisfied
by extra imports will lead to greater inflationary strains than
one which is, though the pace of inflation will be influenced
both by the degree of flexibility in the economy and by other
factors, such as whether an incomes policy is in operation. The
crucial point, however, is that although the pace at which the
government deems it safe to expand will be determined by these
domestic factors, it will not be determined—or not nearly so
much as it would be in the absence of import and exchange
controls—by external factors. Import controls will inhibit the
emergence of a balance of payments problem on current
account, and exchange controls will prevent or at any rate
mitigate any run on the currency, in response to lower interest
rates or the expectation of a higher inflation rate, that would
otherwise force the government to abandon its expansionary
policies.[1]

Attractive though such a scenario must seem to any country
inhibited from expanding by potential balance of payments
problems or pressures on its currency, there are a number of
serious difficulties about such a strategy. These will be briefly
discussed in roughly ascending order of importance.

First, severe transitional problems may be encountered by a country seeking to introduce a system of import and exchange controls. Such a system cannot easily be constructed overnight, and the knowledge that the government is constructing it—even the suspicion that it is planning to construct it—may precipitate the very financial crisis it is designed to avoid. This is particularly true of exchange controls, since such very large sums of money can be moved out of the country's currency at very short notice. The British exchange control apparatus abolished in October 1979, for example, had been erected at the time of the outbreak of the Second World War, when the world was much less interdependent than it is today, and when the government's ability to take draconian action was enhanced by the national emergency. It is difficult to see how similar action could be taken in peacetime—or how the 600 exchange control jobs abolished by the Bank of England in October 1979 could be restored—sufficiently rapidly to prevent a severe, and perhaps politically fatal, run on the currency. If ever there is a danger of the horse bolting before anyone has time to lock the stable door, this seems likely to be it.

A second problem—even if these transitional difficulties are successfully overcome—relates to the effectiveness of a system of exchange controls (import controls are easier to administer and police). Of their very nature, exchange controls on outward capital flows create a demand for foreign exchange that is unsatisfied at the existing exchange rate. From this develops a lower, unofficial, exchange rate for the country's currency, which may be fostered or condoned by the authorities (as in the case of Britain's former 'investment dollar' market), or may simply be a black market rate. Whichever is the case, the existence of two separate exchange rates for the same currency leads to strong arbitrage pressures, since there is a profit to be made by buying foreign currency at the official exchange rate and selling it in the unofficial market where it is at a premium. Particularly at times of crisis, this arbitrage will put downward pressure on the official exchange rate—one of the things exchange control was designed to avoid. Moreover, the existence of a black market in the country's currency will diminish the extent to which it can protect its reserves: to take a familiar example from Italian experience, suitcases of its currency notes smuggled out of the country are liable to end up being presented to its central bank for redemption as foreign exchange. In short, there is an inherent incentive for people and businesses to evade exchange controls, and the complexity of today's international financial relationships affords a variety of opportunities for such evasion. That it is possible for advanced countries with sophisticated administrative machinery to operate exchange control regimes is indicated by the experience until relatively recently of such countries as Britain and France. But the costs are high, and the results imperfect.

A third problem is more controversial, but also more fundamental, since it concerns the consequences of the reduction in competition in the home market which will follow the imposition of import controls. One effect of imposing controls on imports of finished manufactures—which is what proponents of the strategy have mainly in mind—is a reduction in the range of choice available to domestic consumers, which would generally be reckoned a reduction in their welfare. This reduction in welfare is the greater, the lower the availability of substitutes for the goods and services no longer offered to the domestic consumer. (The biggest welfare losses may attend not import controls as such, but exchange controls which involve a maximum foreign travel allowance, like the £50 per year allowance imposed in Britain in 1966, or the 2000 franc allowance imposed in France early in 1983: there are no close substitutes for foreign travel.) The argument of proponents of the strategy is that these undoubted welfare losses are swamped by the welfare gains resulting from the higher level of output and employment made possible by import controls. But there is no objective way of assessing whether or not this is so. A second crucial question is whether the effect of import controls will be to make domestic industry more or less efficient. Proponents of the strategy argue that the assurance of a protected home market will enable domestic manufacturers to reap the economies of scale that undoubtedly exist in much of industry, and will give the confidence to engage in ambitious investment programmes which will lead to increases in productivity not otherwise attainable.[2] Sceptics take the view that less competition will mean lower productivity and less efficiency. Certainly it is difficult for any observer of, say, the British motor industry in recent years (or even the American motor industry) to believe that an import ban on foreign cars would have *increased* the efficiency of British Leyland (or General Motors); the opposite effect seems much more plausible.

The possibility that other nations will retaliate against a country which imposes import and exchange controls constitutes a fourth, and major, problem. For developed countries, import controls are effectively outlawed by GATT—and for those countries which belong to the EEC, by Community legislation. Exchange controls, somewhat more ambiguously, are discouraged by the IMF. A country which breaks the rules of the game can hardly complain if others take action to discriminate against it. The Cambridge Economic Policy Group has argued that, in the event of Britain unilaterally imposing controls on imports of manufactured goods, it would be illogical for other countries to retaliate by discriminating against British exports. For one thing, other countries presumably buy British exports because they represent the best value for money; why should they reduce their own welfare by switching to higher cost or lower quality goods from other sources? More generally, since the purpose of British import controls would be to permit an increase in the country's level of employment and growth rate, it would only be for a few transitional years that Britain's imports would be lower than they otherwise would have been; after that, though still constrained below the level Britons would like to buy, they would be at a higher absolute level than they would have been without the import control strategy. Thus, after the first few years, world exports to Britain would be higher than they otherwise would have been, and other countries should have no complaints. This chain of reasoning, though logically impeccable, is psychologically flawed. It is very difficult to believe that other governments are going to respond to the accounting arithmetic of the argument rather than to the political pressures from their affected industries. There would seem a strong likelihood of retaliation against British exports that would reduce—perhaps eliminate altogether—the gains to output and employment resulting from the controls on imports. Indeed at a time of world recession, when national governments are already under heavy pressure to protect sectors of the economy threatened by foreign competition, the imposition of import controls by any major trading nation is less likely to evoke a calm and understanding response from other countries than it is to set in motion a chain-reaction of escalating import barriers around the world.

This last consideration points to what probably constitutes the biggest difficulty of all about a strategy of de-linking. The strategy may—depending on the answers to the series of questions just discussed—represent an optimal policy for a single country. But if all the countries whose expansion has been inhibited at various times over the past decade by the deflationary bias at work in the international economy were to opt for a strategy of de-linking, the consequent fall in world trade, output and investment would probably by very severe indeed. It is true that countries such as Germany and Japan would be unlikely of their own accord to opt for such a strategy. Although, as was seen earlier, even they have been inhibited in their economic policies by the effects of high interest rates in the United States, they have both benefitted so much from the free world trading regime, and seem so likely to go on doing so in the future, that any systematic de-linking from the international economy on their part appears very unlikely. The same cannot, however, be said of a number of other European countries such as Britain, France, Italy and perhaps some of the Scandinavian countries; nor, necessarily, of the United States. If these countries were to opt for a strategy of de-linking, the retreat within OECD from the present regime of fairly unrestricted free trade and capital flows would be very marked. Moreover, in this event, even Germany and Japan (the latter already a country with an unenthusiastic attitude to imports of manufactured goods) would probably be forced to resort to a greater degree of protectionism. The process would be cumulative: individual countries would find their export markets disappearing, and in order to protect their balance of payments and create new employment for those who lose their jobs in the export industries they would further tighten import and exchange controls, leading to further job losses in other countries—and so on. In the short run at least, it is hard to doubt that the effects of a process of this kind would be even more severe for the OECD economy—and therefore for the rest of the world as well—than anything that has happened since the same kind of process occurred in the 1930s.

In the longer run, the effects are not so clear. As countries adapted, shifting resources from exports to import substitutes, the fall in output and employment would be reversed, and the advantages of a lower degree of dependence on events and policies elsewhere would begin to make themselves felt. Many of the gains from international trade—one of the factors which have led to the present degree of interdependence in the world economy—would, it is true, have been lost. But how far this would really matter is a contentious issue. The rapid growth of international trade over the past thirty or forty years has not primarily been of the classic nineteenth-century type, where countries with a comparative advantage in manufacturing export manufactured goods in exchange for food and raw materials from countries whose comparative advantage lies in these primary products. It has mainly consisted in the growth of trade in manufactured goods: typically, individual OECD countries have increased their exports *and* imports of chemicals, machinery, transport equipment and so on. Though some of the reasons for this may be good economic ones, many of them simply reflect the pursuit of rising sales and profits by increasingly large and powerful multinational corporations, and should not be treated with undue respect by national governments concerned with the welfare of their citizens. The most casual consumer in the average OECD country must continually be observing that he is buying goods made abroad which are virtually identical to goods which are—or were, or could be—made at home. It may well be that in some immediate and static sense the foreign good costs less than the home good, and that the consumer benefits from his ability to buy it. But if the consumer's ability to buy the cheaper foreign good requires a free international trading and financial system with the kind of deflationary bias described above, this immediate and static comparison of cost may be misleading. The consumer may be better off—he himself may be employed rather than unemployed—if he lives in a country in which he has to buy the more expensive home-produced good, but in which there is a higher level of output and employment.

The verdict on the long-term consequences of de-linking must remain an open one. There is no means of knowing what the effects on employment and real incomes in particular countries would be; and even if there were, different people would evaluate the outcome differently, depending on their own attitudes and preferences, and the relative importance they attach, for example, to security of employment compared with range of choice of consumer goods. These long-term consequences of a de-linked system, however, must be re-garded as of little more than academic interest if the short-term consequences of moving to such a de-linked system are unacceptably high. If, for example, the short-term costs of de-linking, in terms of falling output and rising unemployment, were so severe as to threaten massive social unrest and, perhaps, the overthrow of democracy in some major OECD countries, then it seems safe to say that it is a course which few of the citizens and none of the governments of those countries would wish to pursue: better, one may feel, to go on muddling along as we have been doing. Unfortunately it is just this muddling along, in a highly interdependent world economic system characterised by a deflationary bias, that has led to the stagnant output and increasingly heavy unemployment of the early 1980s. Muddling along may no longer be enough. This brings us to consideration of the second possible strategy identified at the beginning of this chapter —a greater degree of international co-ordination of national economic policies.

The governments and central banks of the main OECD countries do engage —as they have done for many years —in periodic discussions of their own and each others' economic policies. There are the annual meetings of the World Bank and International Monetary Fund, the six-monthly meetings of the IMF Interim Committe, and quarterly meetings of central bank governors under the auspices of the Bank for International Settlements. For Britain, there are the annual meetings of the Commonwealth Finance Ministers; for the ten members of the European Econo-mic Community, frequent meetings of ministers and offi-cials at Brussels. Most important of all, perhaps, are the regular meetings of ministers, and even more frequent meetings of officials, at a series of OECD committees and working parties in Paris. At all these meetings governments explain and justify their own economic policies, and sometimes criticise those of others. But this process in no way represents a *co-ordination* of these economic policies. Governments do, of course, take note of what other governments are doing or planning to do, since, as was emphasised in Chapter 2, in a highly interdependent world expected developments in other countries are necessarily a vital input into a government's economic forecasts, on which its own policy decisions are based. But these policy decisions are still taken almost exclusively with a view to their effect on the country's own output, unemployment, inflation and other key economic variables. The adverse effects which these decisions may have on other countries may occasionally be analysed and criticised by others; but such criticism is very rarely heeded.

The international co-ordination of national economic policies would involve a significant step forward from present procedures. Governments would have to be willing to modify their own economic policies, taking action they would not otherwise have taken, in order to reduce the adverse effects (or increase the favourable effects) on others —on the understanding that other governments were willing to do the same. Instead of making major policy decisions on a unilateral basis, governments would, in effect, engage in multilateral negotiations with the governments of other major countries, seeking to reach agreement on the policies to be pursued by each. No government would be forced to adopt policies against its will, so no question of an infringement of national sovereignty would arise. But each government would agree to submit its policy proposals to the scrutiny and comments of other countries before making final decisions, encouraged to do this by the knowledge that the inhibitions the procedure would impose on its own freedom of action would be matched by the greater influence it would acquire over the decisions of others.

The overwhelming argument in favour of such international co-ordination of national economic policies is that it would permit a greater degree of expansion for OECD countries, and thus for the world economy as a whole: output would be higher, growth faster and unemployment lower. This would occur because individual countries would have less reason to fear that expansionary measures would lead to balance of payments deficits and pressure on their currencies or foreign exchange reserves. Simultaneous expansion by other countries would help to ensure that a particular expanding country's exports rose as well as its imports, thus minimising its balance of payments problems, and affording the world financial community no particular reason to opt out of its currency and into others.

Up to a point, expansion of the world economy can be regarded as a 'public good', as an analogy may serve to illustrate. A simple example of a public good is street lighting. Such lighting will not be provided by market forces: it will not pay any individual resident of a street to install lighting, since the small fraction of the total benefits which will accrue to him is unlikely to exceed the costs of installation. For the residents of the street taken as a whole, however, the benefits may well exceed the costs, so that —provided the costs can be shared equitably among the residents —everybody would be better off if the lighting were installed. The inability of the unco-ordinated decision-making process of the market to deal with this problem typically leads to another solution: local (or central) government. The local authority undertakes the expense of installing and operating street lighting, covering the costs by levying taxes of one sort or another on the residents. In theory at least, everyone is better off for this organising activity of local government.[3] The same kind of principle applies to economic expansion in an interdependent world. It may not pay any individual country to expand, since many of the benefits, in the form of higher output and employment, may accrue to other countries whose exports to the home country will now increase, whereas the costs, in the form of a loss of confidence in its currency or outflow of foreign exchange, are borne by the expanding country alone. But if a significant number of countries expand simultaneously, the benefits to each country are likely to exceed the costs. The mechanism for organising this simultaneous expansion cannot, of course, be the same as in the case of street lighting, since there is no prospect of a world government which could supply public goods to sovereign nation-states in the way that local government supplies public goods to the residents of a particular area.

But provided the number of countries is fairly small—the six or eight main OECD countries, for example—there is no reason why a similar effect should not be produced by negotiations among them, just as street lighting could in principle be provided as a result of negotiations among the residents of a small housing estate comprising only six or eight houses.

There are two respects in which a greater co-ordination of national economic policies, if it could be achieved, might be thought to score over de-linking as a way of dealing with the deflationary bias at work in the international economy. One is that it would be entirely consistent with the retention—indeed the expansion—of the gains from trade which have accrued from the relatively free flow of goods and capital from one country to another. As was indicated earlier, one may be sceptical of the extent to which the kind of international specialisation which has attended the rapid growth of world trade over the past few decades has in fact increased welfare; but in so far as it has—and it can be argued that only through international trade can countries benefit from *both* economies of scale *and* a wide diversity of consumer goods—then international co-ordination of macroeconomic policies which permits the continued free play of market forces can preserve these welfare gains in a way that de-linking clearly cannot. Secondly, unlike de-linking, which requires individual countries to erect formidable systems of import and exchange controls, greater policy co-ordination does not demand significant organisational or institutional change. It could be achieved through the medium of existing institutions, the OECD in Paris being the obvious forum for the necessary discussions and negotiations.

Two main objections may be raised to the notion that greater policy co-ordination can provide a satisfactory antidote to the deflationary bias inherent in the present interdependent world economy. One of these has validity only within certain limits. The other does represent a genuine difficulty, though by no means an insuperable one.

The first objection is that, in recent years at any rate, what has inhibited individual OECD governments from pursuing more expansionary policies has not been the likely consequences for their balance of payments, but the likely consequences for their inflation rate. In so far as this is true, the international co-ordination of economic policies proposed here is irrelevant to the factors which have been holding back expansion. Indeed—it could be argued—it is' worse than irrelevant, since to the increasing pressure of demand in domestic goods and labour markets attending expansion in individual countries would be added the likelihood of a boom in world commodity prices. The great commodity price boom of 1971–73, after all, which had a significant inflationary impact on the world economy, was mainly the result of the coincidence that, for almost the first time since the war, virtually all OECD countries were expanding rapidly at the same time.[4] To attempt deliberately to engineer a co-ordinated expansion of the main OECD countries would be to re-ignite the rapid inflation of the 1970s, and nullify the sacrifice of output and employment sustained in the late 1970s and early 1980s in the pursuit of a long-term solution to the problem of inflation.

In its most fundamentalist form, this objection to the international co-ordination of economic policies with a view to a general expansion can hardly be countered, since it reflects a set of values hostile to *any* increase in inflation, regardless of the corresponding benefits in terms of higher ouput and lower unemployment. Since it cannot be denied that an expansion of output in OECD countries rapid enough to help bring down unemployment from the very high levels of the early 1980s might be attended by *some* increase in the inflation rate, such an expansion must necessarily be ruled out by the fundamentalists, and with it the co-ordination of economic policies needed to create it.

It is, however, implausible to ascribe governments' reluctance to take expansionary measures wholly or even mainly to this kind of fundamentalist attitude of inflation. As was illustrated in detail in Chapter 6, at one time or another over the past decade all the main OECD countries have been inhibited or prevented from pursuing expansionary policies which they favoured on domestic grounds by the threat or onset of balance of payments problems on current account, or capital account, or both. It is of course true that a crucial factor in the outflow of capital was often the world financial community's belief that the government's expansionary policies would lead to faster inflation and a weakening current account, that this in turn would lead to an outflow of capital which would depress the exchange rate, raise import prices and thus give a further twist to the inflationary spiral; and that—to make the prophecy fulfil itself—the thing to do was to get out of the currency in question as soon as possible. But this inhibiting mechanism on expansion is quite different from the fundamentalist one just referred to. In the fundamentalist scenario, the government itself is assumed to reject expansion for fear that it would lead to some increase in inflation. In this scenario, the government chooses expansion but is prevented from pursuing it by the reactions of the world financial community. In the fundamentalist scenario, co-ordination of economic policies is irrelevant. But in this one it is highly relevant. If all the main countries are expanding together, this not only helps individual countries to avoid the current account deficits which are one of the factors leading to an outflow of capital, but lessens the vulnerability of any given currency to destabilising speculation. The world financial community has no particular reason to get out of one currency and into another. The danger, for any individual country, of a falling exchange rate interacting viciously with a rising inflation rate is significantly diminished.

Thus it would seem that it has not been simply the fear of the direct effects on inflation that has inhibited OECD governments from pursuing expansionary policies, but the likely consequences for the balance of payments and the exchange rate. If this was true of the late 1970s, it is likely to be even more true of the early 1980s. The general fall in inflation and rise in unemployment have shifted the balance, weakening the argument for resisting expansion because it may lead to some rise in the inflation rate; and in any case the fall in inflationary expectations and the large amount of· unemployment and spare capacity in OECD economies in the early 1980s suggest that there may be a good deal of scope for several years ahead for productivity to rise at a rate which may approximate the rise in money incomes, permitting real wages to rise at an acceptable rate without setting off a new bout of inflation.

None of this means that the inflationary consequences of a set of internationally co-ordinated expansionary policies should be dismissed. The heavy unemployment and widespread spare capacity characterising the world economy in the early 1980s may be a misleading guide to how much expansion is feasible: the unemployed may lack the skills which rising output would require; the capacity may be obsolete. Some aspects of this problem are discussed in the next chapter. Similarly, the low supply elasticities of many primary products may mean that a rapid expansion of output in OECD countries would lead to a boom in commodity prices which, if not of 1971–73 proportions, could be disruptive enough. But—unless one assigns virtually no importance to high employment and rising real incomes—this cannot be taken as an absolute argument against a co-ordinated expansion. The costs of expansionary policies in terms of higher inflation must be measured against the benefits in terms of rising output and employment. At most, the fear of inflation may be an argument for erring on the side of caution rather than recklessness in deciding on the scale of the expansionary policies to be adopted. It cannot be regarded as a reason for making no attempt to overcome the deflationary bias in the working of the international economy.

Of course, the extent to which individual countries will in fact adopt expansionary policies, if international co-ordination removes or weakens the balance of payments constraints on doing so, will vary. Values differ: different governments will assign different degrees of importance to low unemployment compared with low inflation. Models of the national or international economy will differ: different governments will have different views about what the inflationary consequences of a given degree of expansion will actually be. This means that, despite the general relaxation of balance of payments constraints implicit in a co-ordinated expansion, some countries will refuse to expand their own domestic demand as much as other countries would like them to. This cannot be helped. It simply means that the degree of expansion of output and reduction in unemployment that can be achieved by international co-ordination will be less than some countries would like. It will nevertheless be greater—perhaps considerably greater—than what can be achieved without such international co-ordination. Half a loaf is better than no bread.

The second main objection that can be raised to the idea of the international co-ordination of economic policies relates not to its desirability, but its workability. For one immediately comes up against what is known as the 'free rider' problem.

The nature of this problem can be illustrated by reference to the street lighting example cited earlier. If street lighting is provided, all residents of the street benefit, whether they contribute to the cost or not: there is no way that any particular resident can be excluded from these benefits on the grounds that he has not contributed to the costs. Provided that he is fairly sure that street lighting is going to be supplied, therefore, each resident has an incentive to minimise his share of the cost, for example by claiming that he is not in favour of street lighting and refusing to play. In other words, he attempts to get a 'free ride.' Much the same applies in an international context. Provided it can be fairly sure that other countries are going to adopt expansionary measures, it will often be in the interests of an individual country to minimise the expansionary measures it adopts itself. It will benefit from the stimulus to its output and employment provided by rising exports to other, expanding economies, without incurring the rising imports that would follow domestic expansionary measures of its own. Its balance of payments will strengthen and its exchange rate will tend to rise, exerting a downward pressure on its inflation rate and earning it the continued respect of the world financial community. If it gets the balance right, such a country may thus achieve a combination of falling unemployment and falling inflation which will be less attainable by other countries which have expanded domestic demand.

There are a number of ways in which a particular country might try to achieve such a favourable combination of objectives. One would be to claim, in the course of the kind of international negotiations suggested above, that its preferences between price stability and expansion were different from what they really were. Reducing or eliminating inflation is our paramount objective, it might—falsely—declare; and no risks can be taken with expansionary measures until this objective is secured. Given the need to respect the internal objectives of sovereign governments, other countries might feel they had no option but to acquiesce in the lack of expansionary measures by this particular government, while still seeing benefits in going ahead with expansionary measures of their own.

A second ploy open to a country wishing to adopt the role of free rider would be to agree that its preferences between price stability and expansion were much the same as everyone else's, but to claim—falsely—that its model of its own economy demonstrated that rather a little domestic expansion would generate rather a big increase in the inflation rate. It might thus seek to persuade other countries that it—unlike them—could afford to contribute very little to a co-ordinated economic expansion. A third approach would simply be to claim that its economic forecasts showed that a substantial domestic expansion was already in the pipeline, as a result perhaps of rising consumers' expenditure or private investment, and that therefore—unlike other countries—no further stimulus was needed from discretionary fiscal or monetary policy.

A good deal could in fact be done to counter these ploys—particularly the last two. The OECD secretariat already makes its own forecasts of the short-term prospects in individual member countries, and these forecasts—the expertise behind them strengthened or expanded if necessary—could be used as ammunition against biased forecasts produced by governments themselves. Much the same applies to exaggerated government claims about the inflationary impact of expansionary measures in its own economy: the national model could be challenged by reference to the OECD model. Spurious government statements about its preferences between price stability and expansion are inherently more difficult to cope with, since such statements purport to reflect value judgments and are thus not susceptible to technical criticism; but there may well be scope for contrasting the government's stance in international negotiations with its pronouncements at home or the clear priorities of its own public opinion.

These responses notwithstanding, the free rider problem cannot simply be dismissed. Even if no country, of its own accord, wished to play the role of free rider, the suspicion that others are doing so may prompt it to do so itself. To put it in more familiar terms, what is involved is a form of multilateral bargaining, in which it is in the interests of each participant to maximise the concessions made by others while minimising those made by itself. Up to a point at any rate, the more expansion a country can get other countries to agree to, and the less it agrees to itself, the better off it is likely to be. Nevertheless, in spite of the apparently irreconcilable demands and unwillingness to make concessions on display at the outset, multilateral bargaining procedures usually do produce results that are agreed to by all the participants, and therefore presumably benefit all the participants in some degree. There is no reason why the same should not be true of the kind of bargaining among the main OECD countries that is at issue here. The more a country tries to get a free ride by adopting the sort of ploys listed above, the greater the likelihood that other countries' suspicions will be aroused, and that they will adopt the same kind of tactics. This creates the danger—just as if all the residents of a street declared themselves firmly opposed to the provision of street lighting—that the public good in question will not be supplied at all: no country will be willing to adopt expansionary measures, and the benefits which would have accrued to everyone will accordingly be foregone. The hope must be that governments will recognise this danger, and refrain from attempting to get a free ride. Thus the free rider problem, though a complication, should not represent a fatal objection to the international co-ordination of economic policies.

*

This chapter has argued that there are two main ways in which OECD countries might reasonably respond to the deflationary consequences of present decision-making procedures, which ignore the external effects of national decisions in a way that might havé been legitimate twenty years ago, but is much less so in the highly interdependent world of the early 1980s. One way is for a country to de-link in some degree from the international economic system, reducing the extent to which its key variables are influenced by policies and developments in other countries, and by the views of the world financial community, and increasing the extent to which these variables can be determined by the government's own policy instruments. The other way is to co-ordinate economic policy more closely with other countries, so that the external effects of national decisions in an interdependent world can be taken more explicit account of, and in particular so that the inhibitions to expansionary policies in one country can be relaxed by agreement on expansionary policies in other countries. Both approaches have advantages and disadvantages, but the tenor of the argument has been that on balance the disadvantages of a de-linked system—and particularly of the process of transition from the present degree of interdependence to a de-linked system—might be the greater. But before trying to reach any final conclusion on this it is necessary to turn to the other dimension in which the contemporary economic decision-making process fails to take proper account of externalities—the temporal dimension. Just as national economic policy decisions largely ignore the effects on other countries, so also do they largely ignore effects which lie more than a few years ahead. And conclusions about how best to cope with this second problem may have implications for conclusions about how to cope with the first.

8 The Future of Employment

As was pointed out in Chapter 2, macroeconomic decisions typically have a relatively short time-horizon—much shorter than the time-horizon of many microeconomic decisions, whether in the public or private sector. Decisions on whether to construct a new power station or natural gas pipeline, or whether to increase the number of university places available for medical students, need to be taken on the basis of conditions expected to obtain in ten or even twenty years' time. Decisions intended to influence the level of unemployment or the rate of inflation or the balance of payments, on the other hand, are generally taken with an eye on their effects in no more than two or three years' time. This difference in time-horizons is perfectly rational: a decision to build a power station or train a doctor has no effect on the supply of electricity or the number of qualified doctors for a decade or so, whereas changes in fiscal or monetary policy have most of their effect on macroeconomic variables within two or three years—indeed sometimes within a matter of months. Thus decisions of the first kind *must* look a decade or more ahead; decisions of the second kind are right in focusing on the next year or two.

It has, of course, always been recognised that macroeconomic policies designed to influence target variables in the short run may also have effects on target variables in the longer run. The main and most obvious effects of changes in fiscal or monetary policy on such key variables as unemployment, inflation and living standards may be felt within a year or two, but there may be other effects which will not show up until much later. Future living standards depend largely on a country's rate of economic growth, and although the factors determining this rate of growth are complex and sometimes mysterious, one important element appears to be the level and pattern of investment, and another the amount and quality of education and training with which a country provides its labour force.[1] Thus if macroeconomic policies designed to influence key variables in the short run have, as a by-product, effects on investment or training, they are likely to have some effects on living standards in the longer run. The restrictive fiscal and monetary policies pursued by most OECD countries in the early 1980s are a case in point. The primary objective of these policies was the short-term one of bringing down the rate of inflation. There is, however, much evidence to suggest that the high level of unemployment and spare capacity and the squeeze on firms' cash flow to which these restrictive policies gave rise had the general effect of reducing expenditure on both investment and training. In West Germany, for example, investment in manufacturing fell by 7 per cent in 1981, and another 7 per cent in 1982.[2] In Britain the number of apprentices taken on by the engineering industries fell in 1982 by 30 per cent compared with 1981—itself the worst year on record.[3] Cuts of this kind in investment and training expenditures are likely to have an adverse effect in the future on the productive potential of OECD countries, and hence the living standards of their people. Moreover, in so far as workers seek to resist these implications for their living standards by battling for bigger money wage increases, future inflation is likely to be higher. And where—as in Britain—education and training have been cut back in response to—or as part of—the government's restrictive fiscal and monetary policies, the consequent increase in the proportion of the labour force that lacks modern skills is likely to mean higher levels of unemployment in the future.

It might be said, then, that macroeconomic policy generates certain temporal externalities—i.e. effects on key variables which lie outside the time-scale being considered by those who are formulating the policy. The policy-makers might be accused of suffering from a form of myopia in ignoring these externalities, concentrating on the short-term effects of their policy measures and taking little or no interest in the effects a decade ahead. Yet this myopia can be defended on at least two grounds. First, the future is so uncertain that no one can know the size, or sometimes even the direction, of the effects of today's measures on key macroeconomic variables a decade hence. The kind of policy-induced recession alluded to above, for example, may have an adverse impact on growth and future living standards through the cuts in investment and training that it leads to, but this adverse impact could conceivably be partly offset, or more than offset, by other factors, such as the effects of a recession in weeding out inefficient producers, reducing restrictive labour practices, and generally creating a more competitive business climate. If there is no agreement on whether the temporal externalities are positive or negative it is not surprising or unreasonable that they should be ignored.

A second, and in practice very powerful, justification for the traditionally short-term focus of macroeconomic policy is that a country's citizens typically display a high rate of time preference, being much more interested in the level of unemployment, inflation and living standards in the present than the level these variables may attain in ten years' time. Democratically elected governments cannot afford to ignore these preferences.

However, the fundamental justification for the short-term focus of macroeconomic policy lies not so much in the argument that the more distant effects of today's policy measures are difficult to predict, nor in the argument that governments are bound to have at least half an eye on their prospects at the next election. It lies, rather, in the basic presumption that much the greater part of the effects of macroeconomic policy measures are felt within two or three years. Thus there is a general presumption that policy measures adopted in 1983, for example, will have most of their impact in or around 1985, and will have very few implications indeed for the level of key target variables in 1995. The corollary of this presumption is, of course, that it will be time enough to worry about 1995 in 1993.

The question which needs to be considered is whether this presumption is still valid, or whether there has been an increase in what we have called temporal externalities so that a satisfactory level of target variables a decade or two ahead is significantly more dependent than it used to be on decisions made today. If there were reasons for supposing this to be the case, then macroeconomic decisions should in principle be taken on the basis of a much longer time-scale than they actually are. Just as greater spatial interdependence requires governments to consider the effects of their actions on other countries, so would greater temporal interdependence require them to consider the effects of their actions on their own citizens a decade or more ahead.

There are two particular sets of developments which must raise doubts about the continuing validity of the traditional short time-horizon of macroeconomic policy. The rest of this chapter discusses the first of these; the second is taken up in the next chapter.

The first set of developments lies in the contemporary technological revolution represented in particular by advances in microelectronics. If, as some fear,[4] the widespread application of this new microelectronic technology leads to a displacement of labour much too large to be absorbed elsewhere in the economy, the rate of unemployment a decade hence will be principally determined not by the macroeconomic policies being pursued at the time, but by developments which are taking place now. It can be argued, in other words, that technological developments are leading inexorably to an unacceptably high rate of unemployment a decade or so in the future, and that orthodox macroeconomic policies pursued at that time will be powerless to reduce it: fiscal and monetary policy will still be able to increase effective demand, but the extra output of goods and services generated by this increase in demand will, in effect, be produced by robots and computers and not by men. One could, indeed, draw an analogy with one of the consequences of greater *spatial* interdependence, which is that if one country increases effective demand but others do not, there may be little increase in its own level of employment, since the supply elasticities of its trading partners collectively are likely to be considerably higher than its own supply elasticities, with the result that a large proportion of the increase in effective demand will be met by imports. Similarly, the spread of microprocessor technology throughout both manufacturing and service sectors threatens the possibility that even a co-ordinated increase in effective demand by all major OECD countries will lead to little increase in employment because little extra direct labour is required to produce a higher level of output. If this kind of scenario is accepted, then it is clear that the traditional short-term focus of macroeconomic policy is no longer appropriate, since such a focus deliberately precludes consideration of a time-scale during which one of the most fundamental objectives of macroeconomic policy—a satisfactory level of employment—must inevitably fail to be achieved.

How far this pessimistic scenario ought to be accepted is a matter of controversy. More optimistic analysts argue that the adverse effects on employment of the new microelectronic technologies have been much exaggerated by a tendency to attribute to the introduction of these technologies the rise in unemployment in OECD countries in the early 1980s, particularly among young people and minority groups, which was in fact simply the effect of a deficient level of demand. In their view, the microelectronic revolution is really no different from other major technological advances which have been made from time to time over the centuries and which have not only been the major factor behind rising living standards in the West but have also led to an overall rise, rather than fall, in employment. On this interpretation, although there may be a disruptive transitional period while the new technology is being introduced, there is little need to fear any longer-term impact on employment.[5]

Although in this stark form these two prognoses are irreconcilable, and only time will tell which is correct, there is in fact a good deal of common ground between the two points of view. There is widespread agreement that in most OECD countries the next decade or two will see a very substantial *gross* displacement of labour by microprocessor and other technologies in both manufacturing and service sectors. At the same time, competition from the newly-industrialising countries of the third world, which often enjoy a combination of modern technology and low labour costs, will continue to eliminate jobs in Western countries. What is really at issue is how far this displacement of labour will be either absorbed by an expansion of employment elsewhere in the economy, or accommodated by a re-definition of the proper relationship between work and leisure; and how far it will simply result in higher involuntary unemployment.

From the point of view of the attainment of society's basic objectives there can be little dispute that the microelectronic chip, like previous technological breakthroughs before it, is in itself a thoroughly good thing. It permits an improvement — in some spheres a very large improvement — in the productivity of labour, and thus opens the way to either an increase in output for the same number of hours worked, or a reduction in the number of hours worked for the same level of output. Unless a zero value is attributed at the margin to both output and leisure, this change must increase a society's welfare. In practice, the increase in labour productivity which has occurred in Western countries over the past century or so has been taken out partly in the form of higher consumption of goods and services and partly in the form of greater leisure. On the basis of past experience, therefore, there is a general presumption that there will be the same response to the increase in productivity to be expected from the widespread introduction of microelectronic technologies. One might expect to see higher levels of per capita consumption, and at the same time an increase in the amount of leisure enjoyed by the average person during his lifetime, whether through a shorter working day or working week, or longer annual holidays, or 'sabbaticals' in the course of an ordinary working life, or earlier retirement, or some combination of all of these. At any rate, this is what would happen in a rational world.

The problem, as the pessimists see it, is that this rational solution is not on offer. The widespread application of microprocessor and associated technology, it is argued, will provide employment for relatively small numbers of highly-qualified people involved in the design, manufacture, installation and maintenance of the new technology, while at the same time eliminating large numbers of mainly semi-skilled jobs in both manufacturing and services. Thus the likely prospect is not one of everyone putting in a somewhat shorter working week or lifetime than before, but of a relatively small number of highly-qualified people being as fully employed as ever, and a relatively large number of people finding themselves unemployed.

If this pessimistic scenario is to prove unfounded, it seems likely that OECD governments will have to adopt new initiatives in three particular spheres of activity, all of which will have implications for the conduct of macroeconomic policy. First, there will have to be a deliberate expansion and encouragement of the labour-intensive sectors of the economy. Secondly, a different approach will have to be adopted towards training and re-training. Thirdly, the relationship between work, leisure and income will have to be re-thought.

As far as labour-intensive employment is concerned, one sector of most OECD economies where there is probably considerable scope for expansion is in small businesses, particularly in the service industries. It is hard to believe that the chip is going to make many inroads into the employment of people in a wide variety of occupations, from house-repairing to hair-dressing, or plumbing to piano tuning. An increase in the number of such businesses (and in some cases in their size—to small from very small) would not only increase employment but would be consistent with the impetus towards greater decentralisation which is beginning to make itself felt in many Western countries, and in accord with the increasing desire of many people in these countries to assume a greater degree of control over their own working environments and working lives. Although market forces themselves will of course be the major factor behind the expansion of such businesses, there is plenty of scope in most OECD countries for greater government encouragement of this process, by more favourable tax treatment, more generous provision of finance or loan guarantees, fewer reporting requirements, and so on.

However the expansion of small businesses is unlikely to provide more than a relatively small proportion of the new jobs that will need to be created if the displacement of labour in prospect in the manufacturing and large-scale private service industries is not to lead to unacceptably high unemployment. It seems probable that a great many of these new jobs will have

to be created within the public sector. In other words, if there is
to be anything like full employment in the traditional sense in
the mid-1990s, the proportion of the labour force working in
the public sector, and the proportion of the national income
accounted for by public expenditure, is likely to be distinctly
larger than it is at present. This proposition is wholly at odds
with the conventional wisdom prevailing in the early 1980s,
and some account of the reasoning behind it is briefly set out
below.

From about the mid-1970s there was a growing backlash
against public expenditure in a number of Western countries,
culminating at the end of the decade in the election of
governments in both Britain and America dedicated to fierce
cutbacks in the size of the public sector. This backlash was in
part an understandable reaction to the rapid growth in public
expenditure as a proportion of the GDP which had occurred in
virtually all OECD countries in the 1950s and 1960s, and which
in Britain continued, under both Conservative and Labour
governments, until the mid-1970s. But it also owed much to
the increasing influence of monetarist and 'supply-side' economics. High public expenditure was a bad thing—according to
this new economic thinking—on one or both of two grounds. If
it was covered by taxation, taxes would need to be so high that
incentives to work and save would be stifled, and the behaviour
and growth of the economy severely impaired. If, on the other
hand, taxation was not high enough to cover expenditure, the
government would have to borrow to make up the difference;
this borrowing would increase the money supply and this
increase in the money supply would worsen inflation.

The experience of the last few years provides little support
for either of these propositions. There has never been much
reason to suppose that the tax levels ruling in the US or even in
Britain have had a serious disincentive effect on work or saving
(technically, that the substitution effect of high marginal tax
rates significantly outweighs the income effect), and certainly
the income tax cuts introduced by both Thatcher and Reagan
Administrations early in their terms of office appear to have
had very little effect of the kind their supply-side advocates had
anticipated. Much the same applies to the other argument: in

both countries (and particularly in Britain during 1979–82) it became apparent that the relationship between the budget deficit (or PSBR), the money supply and the inflation rate was an exceedingly loose and variable one,[6] and accordingly that there was no simple causal relationship between the budget deficit (itself in any case highly dependent on the level of activity in the economy, as was argued on pages 55–59) and the rate of inflation.

Underlying these more explicit and intellectual arguments against high public expenditure, however, were frequently to be caught glimpses of reasoning of a less coherent and more atavistic kind, as instanced by references in government speeches to 'the burden of public expenditure' or 'wasteful public expenditure' on the one hand, in contrast to the virtues of 'the wealth-creating (i.e. private) sector of the economy' on the other. At its most sophisticated, this amounts to no more than the claim that there are a lot of civil servants or federal employees sitting around in Whitehall or in Washington doing very little. If this is so, such waste should of course be eliminated, but the argument provides no justification for shifting resources *from* the public sector *into* the private sector unless one makes the large assumption that there is no comparable degree of inefficiency or wastefulness in the private sector. The terms in which public expenditure is frequently discussed, however, suggest that such expenditure is being condemned at a much more primitive level of thinking. There is a clear implication that the food or clothes or cars produced and marketed by the private sector constitute useful output or 'wealth', whereas the services rendered by public sector employees such as teachers or nurses or firemen or local authority employees do not.[7] This is, of course, simply wrong. There is nothing inherently more valuable about the output of a car worker than the output of a public sector employee, as is evident from the fact that the car worker may prefer—rather than himself owning a second car—to have his wife competently nursed during childbirth, his children properly educated at school, or his elderly mother provided by competent local government employees with rent or rate rebates to which she is entitled. In this example the car worker is implicitly in favour (in a country where, as in Britain, most teaching and nursing is provided through the public sector) of a relatively high level of public expenditure.

It can, of course, be argued that in any given country at any given time the balance between public and private expenditure is different from what its citizens would wish: that, for example, the car worker would prefer to enjoy fewer public services, and pay lower taxes so that he could afford a second car. But such a judgment is notoriously difficult to make: the area of social choice is one of the most intractable in economic theory. There is in practice no occasion on which the car worker—or anyone else—is presented with a clear-cut choice between lower taxes and better public services. Elections contested by left-wing and and right-wing parties may involve some choice of this kind, but invariably involve many other choices as well. Questionnaires or public opinion polls purporting to demonstrate wide support for lower taxation give little confidence that the implications for public services have been fully appreciated by the respondents; and campaigns for lower taxes are often organised or manipulated by the wealthy, who undoubtedly would be unambiguous beneficiaries of cuts in taxes and public expenditure, but who are hardly typical of the nation as a whole. If the balance between public and private expenditure is wrong, in short, we have no assurance that it is in the direction of there being too much public expenditure. Perhaps the car worker would rather pay higher taxes and enjoy better public services.

Whatever view one may take about the correctness or otherwise of the share of public expenditure in the GDP in the typical OECD country in the early 1980s, or the share of public sector employment in total employment, the future imposes its own logic. It is difficult to deny that *if* the microprocessor displaces large numbers of jobs in manufacturing and in many large-scale private service industries, *then* it is only reasonable to expect—and indeed to plan for—an increase in the share of total employment in the public sector by the mid-1990s. This is not just for the negative reason that it is better for people to be employed in the public sector than to be unemployed. It stems from the fact that in many parts of the public sector the very nature of the job or service being performed makes it difficult for productivity to be increased or, indeed, measured. There is a limit, for example, to how far the productivity of a teacher or nurse can be increased—even in the era of the microchip. Larger classes per teacher or more beds per nurse constitute not an increase in productivity but a fall in the quality of the service being provided to the individual student or patient. The same applies, in varying degrees, to a whole host of other central or local government employees—doctors, civil servants, social workers, home helps, policemen, firemen, lawyers, town planners, dustmen, road sweepers, valuers, health and safety inspectors, librarians, playgroup supervisors, gardeners, traffic wardens etc. etc. If there is to be an increase in the level of the services such people provide, comparable to the increased level of output of goods and some private services made possible by the microelectronic revolution, then more people will be needed to provide them. If only a small proportion of the population is needed to produce all the cars, video recorders, space invader machines and other future wonders that people want, it is only rational that the rest of the labour force should be employed in providing the other goods and services on which people place a positive value. Many of these services are provided by the public sector, and an increase in their provision will require an increase in the proportion of the labour force employed in the public sector.

If the first part of a rational response to the prospect of massive job displacement over the next ten or fifteen years lies to some extent in a relative expansion in the size of the public sector, the second part must lie in a major reorganisation and expansion of the content of education and training. The creation of new jobs, whether in the private service or public sectors of the economy, will only be feasible if people are trained to do the jobs created. What must at all costs be avoided is a situation in which large numbers of people are unemployed—whatever macroeconomic policies governments adopt—because they have no skills, or only skills that have been made obsolete by technical progress.

As far as the training of younger workers is concerned, there should be no insuperable difficulties—though it is noticeable that some OECD countries have been considerably more successful at this than others: experience in Germany, where

more than 90 per cent of school leavers receive some form of
vocational training, is in marked contrast with Britain's long-
standing comparative failure to equip its labour force with
modern skills. However it seems likely that many younger
workers, however well trained to operate the new technologies,
will only find employment if a solution is found to the far
knottier problem of providing new employment for the older
workers, whose skills have been rendered obsolete by technological developments, and whom in many cases younger
workers will be displacing. In other words — particularly in
countries like Britain, with strong trade union organisations — it may only be possible to exploit the new technologies
to the fullest advantage if the older workers displaced by the
process are themselves re-equipped in the new skills, or re-
trained to perform other jobs.

This problem will not be easy to solve, particularly in the
case of, say, semi-skilled manual or clerical workers in their
forties — too old to be easily re-trained but too young to be
thinking of retirement. Nevertheless, there is no reason why
many such people should not be successfully assisted to learn
new entrepreneurial or technical skills which would permit
them to start their own small business, or take on some job in
the private or public service sector. The essential prerequisite is
likely to be a commitment to such re-training on the part of
society, and the provision of public finance in order to
implement the commitment. It is society as a whole that
benefits from the increases in productivity made possible by the
introduction of new technologies, and it is in the interests of
society as a whole that those displaced by this process should
find employment elsewhere rather than remain wholly unemployed. Accordingly it is only right that society should finance
the necessary re-training expenditures, and maintain the
individual during the period of re-training. Even on the
narrowest calculation — taking account only of the tax revenue
the Treasury receives from an employed individual and the
social security benefits it pays out to an unemployed one — such
re-training and maintenance expenditures may not look extra-
vagant.[8] When wider social costs and benefits are taken into
account, they are likely to seem eminently justified.

The third response which will need to be made to the

displacement of labour involved in the microelectronic revolution is likely to involve new relationships between work, leisure and income. The 40-hour week, 48-week year, 40-year working life still regarded as the norm in most Western societies is wholly untypical of most of the history of *homo sapiens* — far less typical, for example, than the four or five hours work a week put in by primitive hunting societies.[9] What seems in prospect during the next decade or two is a transition to a much shorter average working life. If this transition is to be satisfactorily accomplished, there must be a widespread willingness to regard a marked increase in leisure time as a blessing rather than a curse, and to accept some changes in the contemporary norms governing the relationship between income and work. In addition to training for work, therefore, advanced industrial countries will need to place much greater emphasis on educating for leisure. School curricula will need to be reorganised and extended, encouraging children to take a pride in developing skills which they will practise not in paid employment, but as part of leading satisfying lives in an age of extensive leisure. This will require the recruitment as teachers of people — some of them no doubt themselves the victims of technological change elsewhere in the economy — with an enthusiastic interest in the whole gamut of human activities from angling to zither-playing. Similarly, increased facilities for developing new interests will need to be provided for adults who wish to make more positive use of their increased leisure time. The evening classes organised by local authorities and many other bodies in Britain may be part of the model here, as may more intensive three-month or nine-month courses of the kind provided by colleges and training institutions of many kinds for mature students seconded for a period by their employer. But the difference would be that the student would be acquiring insights or skills to enable him to enjoy his leisure time more, rather than techniques designed to improve his performance in his job.

*

The implications of this chapter for macroeconomic policy can be fairly briefly stated. No one can know the pace at which microelectronic technology will displace labour in manufacturing or service industries, nor indeed what other technical or other changes the next decade or two hold in store. There is a limit to how far it is useful to try to forecast the future, or to make decisions or commitments in the present on the basis of presumptions about the future which may turn out to be wrong. On the other hand, to ignore what the present appears to be telling us about the future is foolhardy. Developments which are already taking place strongly suggest that over the next decade or two large numbers of workers in Western countries will be displaced, particularly from manufacturing industry, by the spread of microprocessor and associated technologies, as well as by competition from newly-industrialising countries. New jobs—albeit involving fewer lifetime hours of work than has been customary hitherto—will need to be created on a large scale if high levels of involuntary unemployment are not to become a permanent blemish on the face of Western society. But many of these jobs cannot be created by macroeconomic policies of the traditional kind. Increases in effective demand engineered by traditional demand management techniques will call forth an increase in the output of goods and services, but much of this extra output will be produced not by men whose skills are obsolete or non-existent but by robots: the employment elasticity of increases in effective demand will be relatively low. In these circumstances, full employment can only be ensured by a significant degree of long-term forward planning. To a much greater extent than before, society must take a view about the nature of the services it will wish to be consuming in ten years' time, and then take steps to train people in the skills which will enable them to perform these services. This will apply particularly in the public sector, where a large part of the increase in employment will probably need to be located.

There are, of course, great uncertainties involved. But the fact that one cannot know the rate at which labour will be displaced from private manufacturing and service sectors is not a good reason for delaying plans to expand employment in the public sector, for the argument cuts both ways: the rate at which labour is displaced from the private sector (and thus the pace at which society benefits from the productivity increases made possible by the chip) will itself be determined in part by the availability of employment elsewhere in the economy. Similarly, no one can know the 'right' occupational distribution of the labour force within the public sector in ten years' time: this will depend both on changes in society's preferences in the meantime, and on technical developments within the public sector itself. Nevertheless, in cases where training or retraining periods are long, or the time needed to construct new physical facilities is protracted, commitments need to be made well in advance: to revert to an earlier example, the pool of doctors or airline pilots available at a given time, or the capacity of hospitals or airports, typically depend on decisions made at least eight or ten years earlier.

In the case of other skills and facilities less forward planning is needed: to take an extreme example, a decision to increase the employment of people who collect litter from public parks with the aid of a pointed stick can be implemented within weeks or even days. But in many cases—in the private as well as in the public sector—a more or less lengthy period of training or retraining is required to equip people with new skills; and—a point not to be under-estimated—the facilities for training and re-training may themselves take a considerable period to build up. At a time of rapid displacement of existing jobs it is going to be increasingly unsatisfactory to rely for a solution to this problem on either the operation of market forces or a process of macroeconomic policy-making which looks no more than two or three years into the future. Nor is the problem likely to be soluble as long as the prevailing ethos in Western societies is firmly set against an increase in the proportion of national income accounted for by public expenditure.

9 Growth, Pollution and Exhaustible Resources

The previous chapter looked at one particular aspect of the traditionally short time-horizon of macroeconomic policy-making: its failure to ensure, at a time of rapid technological change, that the labour force is equipped with new skills, or that there are fundamental changes in attitude to the relationship between work and leisure, such that a reasonably full level of employment is attainable provided that the appropriate macroeconomic policies are pursued. This chapter goes on to consider some other problems inherent in the short time-horizon of macroeconomic policy.

It is not very surprising that little attention has been paid to the longer-term implications of today's macroeconomic decisions, nor that—to look at it the other way round—little attempt has been made to think out what decisions ought to be made today if conditions in the future are to be satisfactory. As has been stressed earlier, the future is not only difficult to predict, but the more difficult, the further ahead one tries to look. It is hard enough to produce accurate forecasts for two or three years ahead; the value of forecasts of what is likely to happen over the next ten or twenty years, let alone longer, must be in serious doubt.

Bolstering this eminently rational case for not attempting to peer too far into the future has been—at any rate since the idea of progress became implanted in Western societies a century or more ago—the comfortable presumption that things would in any case go on getting better.[1] This notion survived the great depressions of the 1880s and 1930s, and both world wars. Not long after the end of the Second World War, indeed, when it looked as though Keynesian policies had solved the problem of unemployment, it assumed a more explicit form. For the best part of a quarter of a century, from roughly the early 1950s to the mid-1970s, a high rate of growth of GDP was widely regarded in OECD countries as one of the fundamental objectives of economic policy. Constraints on achieving a sustained high rate of growth of GDP were, indeed, much discussed; but they were seen (particularly in countries with relatively sluggish growth rates, such as Britain and, to a lesser extent, the US) in terms of low rates of investment, poor management, inadequate education and training, restrictive practices and the inhibiting effects of overvalued exchange rates. Little attention was paid in either public discussion or the technical economic literature to the kind of constraints that might be imposed by the rising amounts of energy and raw materials required by rapid rates of growth in industrial countries, or the increasing levels of pollution that might be the result. Economic policy was based on the largely unexamined assumption that whatever quantities of energy or material inputs were required to sustain growth into the indefinite future would be forthcoming, and that whatever levels of pollution of land, sea or air might attend ever-rising levels of industrial output could be accommodated or neutralised without undue difficulty. In short, there was a widespread presumption on the part of policymakers—and the populations they represented—that growth was both desirable and feasible.

From about the mid-1960s onwards both these propositions began to be challenged. A challenge to each proposition has, of course, implications for the other: if one takes the view that growth is undesirable, then strictly speaking the question of whether or not it is feasible is of no interest; similarly, if growth is not feasible, then whether or not it is desirable is an academic question. In practice, the two arguments often get intermingled. Nevertheless, for analytical purposes each argument needs to be stated, and examined, separately.

There is a considerable literature, stretching back over a good many years, on the question of how far economic growth, as measured by a steady increase in real GDP, is desirable. From this body of work, one might select three particular books as being especially interesting and influential.

Mishan's book *The Costs of Economic Growth* (1967) can be read as little more than a splendidly passionate and idiosyncratic tirade against all those features of contemporary society which middle-aged, middle-class intellectuals from the hair-shirt tradition so detest: other people's cars, transistor radios, jet flights and so on. But it is based on a compelling piece of economic analysis: the fact that growth of the GDP gives rise to external diseconomies, in terms of pollution, congestion, noise and loss of amenity generally which, not being easily measurable, are largely ignored in decision-making, and are not taken account of in calculating the GDP. 'The growing incidence of the external diseconomies generated by certain sectors of the economy and suffered by the public at large' Mishan regards 'as the most salient factor responsible for the misallocation of our national resources' (p. 85). 'The adoption of economic growth as a primary aim of policy' he argues, is 'as likely to add, at least, as much 'ill-fare' as welfare to society' (p. 64). 'The continued pursuit of economic growth in Western societies' he concludes, 'is more likely on balance to reduce rather than increase social welfare' (p. 219).

Another of Mishan's charges (pp. 157–62) is that the kind of economic growth which takes place in the West has the effect of presenting people with trivial choices (between one gadget and another) while denying them real choice (between one kind of life and another). This point is also made by Scitovsky in his book *The Joyless Economy* (1976), though he develops, with relish, an altogether broader attack on the Western—particularly the American—way of life and its emphasis on economic growth as a crucial policy objective. Drawing heavily on the literature of psychology and physiology, he argues that once the basic needs of food, clothing and shelter are provided for, few of the sources of human pleasure or satisfaction are measured by the GDP. 'The national income' he asserts, 'is, at the very best, an index of economic welfare, and economic welfare is a very small part and often a very poor indicator of human welfare' (p. 145). Scitovsky draws attention to evidence[2] that people's happiness, as assessed by themselves, though fairly closely correlated with their position in the income scale, shows little or no correlation with increases in income over time. In the US, over the period from 1946 to 1970, 'almost twenty-five years, per capita real income rose by 62 per cent, yet the proportion of people who consider themselves very happy, fairly happy, and not too happy has hardly changed at all. Our economic welfare is forever rising, but we are no happier as a result' (pp. 134–5). One might well wonder, on the basis of this evidence, what is the point of economic growth.

Scitovsky's—and others'—observation that happiness is correlated with ranking in the income or status scale rather than with absolute income level was one of the features of contemporary society explored in depth in Hirsch's book *Social Limits to Growth*. Hirsch's basic argument is that as economic growth proceeds and people come increasingly to possess the mass-produced goods (cars, durables etc.) which can be supplied in virtually limitless quantities, they come increasingly to desire other goods and services, such as uncongested roads on which to drive their cars, or country cottages to drive them to, or a level of education that qualifies them for the top jobs. The problem is that not only can these other goods and services not be mass-produced; of their very nature, the more they are sought after by people in general, the less of them is available to the particular individual. 'Addition to the material goods that can be expanded for all', as Hirsch puts it, 'will, in itself, increase the scramble for those goods and facilities that cannot be so expanded' (p. 10). In other words, what Hirsch calls 'positional goods' come to assume greater importance as simpler material needs are satisfied, and positional goods—whether an isolated country cottage or a better education than other people—can by definition only be acquired by a minority. This, Hirsch argues, explains the paradox that as economic growth proceeds and the national income increases, people tend to become less, rather than more, contented; and more, rather than less, concerned with the distribution of income and wealth and 'their relative position in the economic hierarchy' (p. 7). 'So the distributional struggle returns, heightened rather than relieved by the dynamic process of growth' (p. 6).

This very brief summary of three particular books cannot do justice either to the books themselves or to the critical tradition of which they form a part. It does, however, serve to illustrate the fact that the desirability of economic growth is by no means unanimously accepted. The arguments and conclusions of all three books can, of course, be criticised. Thus while one may agree with Mishan that the external diseconomies associated with economic growth may temper the improvement in social welfare resulting from that growth, one may feel it a little extreme to claim that the net effect of growth is actually to *reduce* welfare, though of course this—like so much else in the growth debate—is a matter not so much of fact as of value judgment. Similarly, one may feel that the very subtlety of Scitovsky's and Hirsch's analyses has caused them to lose sight of the simple and obvious benefits that higher real incomes and more leisure time have brought to most people. Nevertheless, it is difficult to read these books without conceding something to the argument that the causes of human happiness and satisfaction are complex and often beyond human control, and that the connection between economic growth and human welfare is frequently tenuous and sometimes perverse.

But for present purposes this is not the point. Whether or not economic growth is regarded as desirable by (often comfortably-off) economists, philosophers or intellectuals generally is a matter of comparatively little importance. The great majority of the population in even the most advanced industrial countries happens to want the higher real incomes that economic growth alone makes possible. There is, to be sure, plenty of scope for argument about the form that economic growth should take. One issue—discussed in the previous chapter in a different context—is how far it should take the form of increased output of the private goods and services purchased by individuals, and how far of the public goods and services provided by central or local government and financed by taxation. Another—particularly contentious—issue discussed later is how far economic growth should rely on the generation of electricity by nuclear reactors. On these and other issues there will continue to be pressures and lobbying by a variety of interested groups—including those who agree with the critics of economic growth. None of this alters the fact that as far ahead into the future as it is useful to look, economic growth—in the sense of a rising real GDP—is going to be desired by the populations of the advanced industrial as well as the developing countries, and is thus going to remain a major objective of economic policy—provided, of course, that it is *feasible*. But is it? To this second, and more complicated, question we now turn.

*

The notion that economic growth might be brought to a halt by a shortage of physical resources has a long history. Almost two centuries have elapsed since Malthus first argued that there was a strong tendency for population to grow faster than the means of subsistence, and it was more than a century ago that Jevons, extending Malthus' insights, predicted, in effect, that economic growth in Britain would soon be brought to an end by the exhaustion of her coal mines.* More recently, a new phase of anxiety about the consequences of continued economic growth was inaugurated by the publication in 1972 of *The Limits to Growth*, a book based on modelling work carried out by Forrester and others at the Massachusetts Institute of Technology, and somewhat grandiloquently subtitled 'A Report for the Club of Rome's Project on the Predicament of Mankind'. This book argued that world population and industrial output per head had been growing exponentially for a century or so, and that if this trend continued (and there was no reason to suppose that it would not), non-renewable resources, such as minerals and fossil fuels, would before long be exhausted—some within the next fifteen or twenty years, most of the others within the next fifty. Rather suddenly industrial production would level out and then plummet downwards, as would agricultural output, by then heavily

---

* According to Keynes, Jevons was also convinced that paper would become increasingly scarce. To guard against this contingency he accumulated such huge quantities of writing-paper and wrapping paper that his children had still not exhausted the stock more than fifty years after his death (Keynes, 1933, p. 117).

dependent on inputs from the industrial sector. Food consumption per head would drop very drastically, the death rate would soar, and there would be a huge fall in world population.

This was the 'standard run'—the most likely result, according to the computer model, of continued economic growth. The modellers were, indeed, willing to examine the consequences of more optimistic assumptions about new resource discoveries, technological breakthroughs on the energy front (including unlimited cheap nuclear power), reduced pollution per unit of output, doubled land yields and 'perfect' birth control (meaning no unwanted children born anywhere after 1975). But it was no good. If resource depletion was avoided, then pollution would get us. If pollution was somehow dealt with, then declining land yields would put an end to us. Catastrophe might be postponed for a few decades, but was still inevitable.

The Limits to Growth soon came under heavy fire from economists and other social scientists.[3] It was pointed out not only that different but equally plausible assumptions about the trends or relationships of particular variables would have led the MIT model to very different results, but also that the model failed altogether to incorporate negative feed-back loops of absolutely critical importance. Increasing scarcity of a resource, for example, leads to a rise in its relative price, an increased search for it, substitution of it by other less scarce resources, greater recycling of existing supplies, and so on. None of this was allowed for by the model; nor indeed was technical progress generally; nor was the way in which the goals and attitudes of people, and the policies of governments, change over time in response to the circumstances and problems that confront them. In short, once a further variable—man—was introduced into the model, the whole picture changed, and the mechanistic projections printed out by the MIT computer ceased to have much meaning.

Unfortunately, it was easier to demonstrate that the MIT projections must be wrong than to formulate projections which must be right. The particular model underlying *The Limits to Growth* might be dead, but some of the issues it raised remained very much alive. A huge literature developed. Some of this (e.g. Olson and Landsberg, 1973, Heilbroner, 1978)—taking, perhaps, the pessimistic view—examined some of the economic and social implications of a low or zero rate of growth.[4] Some of it, on the other hand (e.g. Dorfman and Dorfman, 1972, Dasgupta and Heal, 1979) focused on the economics of resource depletion and environmental pollution, with a view to answering the question of whether these apparently threatening problems were, in fact, so insoluble.

As far as pollution is concerned, it would now be widely accepted among economists that to a considerable extent pollution is not an inevitable concomitant of economic growth, but something which happens as a result of a failure to establish an adequate system of markets, particularly in common property resources. There are no markets in externalities, positive or negative, with the consequence that there is an excessive production of negative externalities and an insufficient production of positive externalities. In principle this problem can be dealt with by a system of taxes and subsidies which 'internalise externalities' by bringing social and private costs and benefits into line with each other. To give a specific example: because businesses are not charged for emitting pollutants into the atmosphere, they produce 'too much' pollution, in the sense that the scale of the firm's output is determined solely by the benefits captured by the firm in the form of sales and profits, and not at all by reference to the costs imposed on others by its discharge of pollutants. In theoretical terms, the firm's scale of output is determined by the intersection of marginal *private* revenue and cost curves, and not marginal *social* revenue and cost curves, and the result will be a higher level of output of goods *and* pollutants than is socially optimal. Thus there is a misallocation of resources. However, this misallocation can in principle be remedied by charging the firm for the negative externalities constituted by the pollution it creates, or—as a proxy for this—taxing its output. The result will be a reduction in its output of both goods and pollutants.

Economic theory, then, has both an explanation of why growth has been accompanied in the past by rising levels of atmospheric pollution, and a remedy for how the problem might be coped with (in so far as it *is* a problem: many people, depending on their values and position in the world income distribution, are likely to prefer more output and more pollution to less pollution and less output; this is one aspect of a general and very important problem discussed later). Systems of taxes and subsidies, it is concluded, can in principle be used to bring social and private costs into line; and if they are difficult to operate in practice, at least the grosser forms of pollution can be dealt with by simple regulation.

Unfortunately, not all of the pollution problem can be written off quite so neatly: there are genuine worries which cannot be allayed by the kind of answers—remedying market failure and improving resource allocation—provided by economists. One such worry is the longer-term effects on the planet of the combination in the atmosphere and oceans of the largely uncontrolled discharge of thousands of man-made chemicals. Another is the longer-term and probably irreversible effect of the building up in the atmosphere of large concentrations of carbon dioxide as a result of the burning of fossil fuels (the so-called 'greenhouse effect').[5] Another is the whole question of nuclear power, and the safe disposal of radioactive waste. These questions are taken up in Chapter 10.

If rising levels of environmental pollution are one consequence of economic growth that people worry about, the other is falling reserves of minerals, fossil fuels and exhaustible resources generally. Although economists may be confident that the feedback effects, via the operation of the price mechanism, of increasing scarcities of resources make wholly unrealistic the kind of scenario painted in *The Limits to Growth*, this by no means implies that the fears of resource exhaustion are groundless.

Uncertainty about the future of exhaustible resources takes two main forms. First, although the planet's stock of exhaustible resources is by definition finite, it is not known what this stock is. Secondly, it is not known what will be the future rate of technical progress. Many forms of technical progress are relevant to the problem: progress in recovering mineral or fossil fuel reserves (deep sea drilling or mining the sea bed); economising on the use of scarce resources (more efficient car engines or house insulation); substituting less scarce for more scarce resources (aluminium for copper); and, more generally, substituting renewable or reproducible resources for exhaustible resources (wind power or solar energy for fossil fuels or, come to that, staircases for escalators). The importance of these mechanisms is very great: it has been demonstrated theoretically, for example, that a decline in people's consumption due to the exhaustion of resources can be postponed indefinitely if one assumes either sufficient possibilities of substituting reproducible capital for exhaustible resources, or a constant rate of resource-augmenting technical progress.[6] It is not clear that either of these assumptions is justified; but neither is it clear that they are not.

There is no way of avoiding this uncertainty. Nevertheless, despite uncertainty, decisions have to be made about the optimal exploitation of exhaustible resources over time. Credit for the first systematic examination of this issue, at least in modern times, is generally attributed to an article published some fifty years ago by Hotelling.[7] Hotelling demonstrated that in a competitive environment, and ignoring extraction costs, the price of an exhaustible resource must rise over time at a rate equal to the rate of interest. It could not rise *more slowly* than the rate of interest, since owners of resource deposits would then sell the resource (or produce more of it) and lend the proceeds—for example by purchasing government bonds—at the prevailing rate of interest. This action would force down the present price of the resource, and increase its rate of growth in the future. Conversely, the price of the resource could not rise *faster* than the rate of interest, since money could then be made by buying stocks of the resource (or producing less)—action which would raise its present price and reduce its future rate of growth. The fundamental implication of the 'Hotelling rule', if one made the important assumption—discussed below—that social and private rates of discount were the same, was that exhaustible resources would be exploited at a socially optimal rate. In other words, exhaustible resources could not be depleted 'too fast'.

While representing a brilliant theoretical insight, the Hotelling rule does not provide easy guidance to what may happen in the real world. (Certainly anyone who had relied on the rule to predict the course of the price of particular exhaustible resources during the half century since Hotelling wrote would probably have burnt his fingers badly.)[8] One problem is that extraction costs are not only positive, but non-linear. Another is that exhaustible resource industries are typically characterised not by conditions of competitive equilibrium, but by a considerable, though varying, degree of monopoly. Hotelling's analysis can, in fact, be relatively easily extended to deal with these two problems.[9] But there is another difficulty which is much more intractable.

This concerns the rate of discount. For exhaustible resources to be exploited at an optimal rate, the Hotelling rule requires that the private rate of discount—the rate at which private firms or individuals discount future profits, income or consumption—should be the same as the social rate of discount—the rate at which society as a whole discounts future income or consumption. However, there are good reasons for supposing that the rate at which private businesses or individuals discount the future is greater than the rate at which society discounts—or *should* discount—the future. Some of these reasons are essentially technical: for example private agents will be interested in the after-tax return on investment, whereas society as a whole is concerned with the before-tax return. This discrepancy will have the effect of raising private rates of time preference relative to the social rate of time preference.

However, there is a more fundamental reason than the discrepancy between pre- and post-tax rates of return for supposing that decisions on investment or resource depletion which are made by private agents will display a higher rate of time preference than the decisions which are made, or ought to be made, by society as a whole. It is perfectly rational for an individual to have a positive rate of time preference—i.e. to prefer a given amount of consumption in the present to the same amount of consumption at some time in the future. This is because he cannot be sure that he will still be there to do the consuming on the future occasion; and indeed if the occasion is delayed long enough, he can be sure that he will not be. Dr Johnson was quite right to eat the best grape on the bunch first, on the grounds that otherwise he might die before getting to it. Private corporations, too, though they may sometimes have a longer time-horizon than the individual, are ultimately answerable for their profits and dividends to shareholders who are individuals. Society, by contrast, outlives any individual—or so it is to be hoped. Thus what is rational behaviour for the individual is not necessarily rational behaviour for society as a whole. In other words, society ought to have a lower rate of time preference, and thus apply a lower rate of discount in its decision-making, than individuals.

Just what the social discount rate ought to be is a complicated question, and depends among other things on the precise numeraire chosen—utility, per capita consumption etc.[10] The utilitarians argued that any discounting of future utilities was morally objectionable, since the happiness of future generations had the same value as the happiness of the present generation; thus the social discount rate should be zero. In principle, much the same conclusion would follow from the adoption of a Rawlsian approach:[11] if everyone ever born or ever going to be born was asked to allocate income or consumption over time, without knowing the time at which they themselves were going to live, it seems likely that they would opt for a constant level of per capita income or consumption over time—in other words that they would demand a zero social discount rate.

One can qualify these arguments in a number of ways, and indeed some utilitarians and others have done so. The doctrine of diminishing marginal utility, for example, implies that if future generations are going to be wealthier than we are, a marginal unit of income or consumption in the future will confer less satisfaction than a marginal unit of income or consumption in the present. This would imply that the correct social discount rate is something greater than zero. By the same token, however, if future generations are going to be poorer than we are (which is what many of those worried about exhaustible resources are afraid of) then society ought to adopt a *negative* social discount rate, assigning *more* importance to future than present consumption. Another qualification is suggested by the possibility that man will not continue to inhabit the planet forever. To take a stark example: if one believed there to be a very high probability that mankind will be obliterated by nuclear war within the next twenty years, there would not be much point in worrying about the rate at which exhaustible resources were being exploited, or in arguing that society ought to have a zero rate of time preference.

These qualifications, however—unless one takes a very pessimistic view about the prospect of a nuclear holocaust—do little to alter the conclusion, at any rate on the basis of a utilitarian or Rawlsian calculus, that the correct social rate of discount is considerably lower than the private rate of discount. Thus one of the requirements of the Hotelling rule for an optimal rate of exploitation of exhaustible resources is not being met. The implication is that exhaustible resources are being depleted too fast.

In so far as this conclusion is accepted, it would seem desirable to search for remedies; and remedies, in principle, there are. It should be possible to devise a system of taxes and subsidies which would bring private and social discount rates into line in exactly the same way that—as was argued earlier—one can in principle devise a system of taxes and subsidies which bring private and social costs into line so as to discourage firms from producing an undesirable amount of pollution. Conservation of mineral or fossil fuel reserves could, for example, be encouraged by subsidies; rates of extraction or depletion could be slowed down by taxes which were high at first and fell as time went on.

It must be recognised, however, that it is not only the skill of the economist or tax expert that would be put to the test by such devices, but the skills of the politician as well. It may in some cosmic sense be right for society to have a low or zero rate of time preference, but politicians are somewhat imperfect interpreters of such cosmic considerations. Perhaps future generations ought to have votes, but in fact they do not. The implication of a very low or zero social discount rate is that consumption in the present should be curtailed in order to permit a high rate of investment and a low rate of resource depletion. This is not a message that democratic governments, faced every few years by the need to hold elections, are anxious to hear. And—an echo of the problems of spatial inter-dependence discussed elsewhere in this book—it would do little good for one government on its own to take a far-sighted view, favouring future voters as much as present ones. If other countries are all depleting exhaustible resources at an excessive rate, it is not rational for any one country to hold back, any more than it is rational for any one motorist to stop using his car because cars pollute the atmosphere with lead.

*

It could, therefore, be argued that exhaustible resources are being exploited too rapidly in the sense that the impact of private rates of time preference which are inappropriately high for decisions made by society as a whole are being insufficiently offset by the collective decision-making process: future generations, in short, are getting a raw deal. But there is no way of proving that this proposition is correct. For one thing, normative judgments are involved, of a kind which cannot be proved or disproved. More to the point, however, is the fact that no one can know what new resource discoveries or technical progress the next ten or fifty or 100 years will bring. To those who claim that exhaustible resources are being exploited too rapidly, or that future rates of economic growth which might be widely regarded as desirable will prove infeasible because of resource exhaustion, another of Keynes' observations about Jevons may seem apposite: 'His conclusions were influenced, I suspect, by a psychological trait, unusually strong in him, which many other people share, a certain hoarding instinct, a readiness to be alarmed and excited by the idea of the exhaustion of resources' (Keynes, *op. cit.*, p. 117).

Nevertheless, the fact that no one has succeeded in demonstrating that economic growth must be reined back if resource depletion is not to lead to catastrophe does not mean that it can be assumed that the rate of economic growth which emerges from all the myriad relevant decisions, including those of traditional macroeconomic policy, is going to have acceptable consequences. The next two chapters consider some more sombre aspects of the problem.

10 The Nature of the Energy Problem

Although the more general scare about resource depletion and environmental pollution sparked off by *The Limits to Growth* receded in the mid-1970s, this did not apply to one crucial dimension of the problem: energy. The other difficulties could probably be coped with, it came to be widely believed, provided that the world could generate sufficient energy, and do so in ways that did not create unacceptable environmental hazards. But could it?[1]

The energy question came into very sharp focus in 1973, when the price of oil rose from around $2 a barrel to more than $10 a barrel—most of the rise occurring in less than three months.[2] It crept upwards over the next few years, and then doubled again in 1979—a bigger rise, in absolute terms, than had occurred in 1973. There were further increases in 1980 and 1981, and by the beginning of 1982 the reference price for light crude was $34 a barrel—*seventeen times* what it had been a decade before. Because of high rates of world inflation, the real oil price (i.e. after deflation by an index of the price of manufactured goods) rose considerably less than this; but even in real terms the price of oil in 1982 was roughly ten times as high as ten years earlier.

This colossal price increase has been seen by some as a dramatic vindication of those who had warned, in the early 1970s, that exhaustible resources were running out. But in fact

130

it was not, at least in any straightforward sense, the effect of the sudden appearance of a shortage of oil reserves of the kind that *The Limits to Growth* had predicted: published proved reserves at the beginning of 1982 in fact represented about thirty-two years' production at the current rate—much the same as at the end of the 1960s.[3] The quintupling of oil prices during 1973 reflected, rather, the sudden coming of age of the OPEC cartel. This organisation had been born more than a decade earlier, but only discovered its strength in the immediate aftermath of the Yom Kippur war, when cutbacks of oil production by Arab countries created something approaching panic throughout the industrialised West. What had happened, in technical terms, was that within quite a short space of time[4] a monopsonistic market structure, in which the major international oil companies, acting in concert, faced and dominated an uncoordinated group of producers was replaced by a situation of bilateral monopoly—one in which two adversaries of roughly equal strength confront each other, and price is indeterminate. Indeed in the short run this description may understate the strength of the producers, because in the short run the price elasticity of demand for oil is very low: consumers have little scope (except by running down stocks) for reducing their purchases of oil, and producers can raise their prices very sharply without much risk of losing sales. The importance of this factor was demonstrated again in 1979. Although the quintupling of the oil price during 1973 had led in the intervening period to many measures of substitution and conservation of the kind economists would expect, the temporary withdrawal from the market in 1979 of one producer (Iran, in the chaos attending the downfall of the Shah) created circumstances—psychological more than physical—in which OPEC could double the price of oil.

Nevertheless, whatever importance one attaches to the institutional fact of the formation and subsequent cohesion of the OPEC cartel, it would be foolish to imagine that a seventeenfold increase in the oil price in the course of a decade is something that can happen in some kind of vacuum. The quintupling of the oil price in 1973 might conceivably be seen as little more than a belated, if abrupt, adjustment to more than a decade of artificially low prices: despite the rapid growth of the world economy in the 1950s and 1960s, oil prices in real terms were 10–20 per cent lower in 1970 than they had been in the mid-1950s.[5] But it is less easy to explain the further trebling of oil prices (from around $11 a barrel in 1974 to around $34 in 1982) in the same way. There is in fact some reason to suppose that in 1970 or thereabouts a fundamental shift occurred in the structure of the world oil market. Crucial to this structural shift was a change in the role of the United States. From having always been more or less self-sufficient in oil, the US, in the late 1960s, rather suddenly became a net importer, relying for supplies not only on traditional sources in the Western hemisphere, such as Venezuela, but also on the Middle East. By the late 1970s it was dependent for as much as half of its supplies on imports. The real effects of this were considerable, since the US accounts for a third of total world oil consumption outside the Sino-Soviet bloc; but the psychological effects, particularly on expectations about oil prices, were probably even greater.

The very big rise in oil prices since 1973, in addition to stimulating the development of new oil fields in such places as Alaska, Mexico and the North Sea, has also led to extensive measures to economise on the consumption of oil, and indeed energy in general. Over the five-year period between 1976 and 1981 OECD GDP rose by 14 per cent, but its primary energy consumption rose by only 1 per cent, and its consumption of oil actually fell by 9 per cent. In some countries particularly dependent on imported energy the decline in the ratio of the volume of energy consumption to GDP was even more marked: in Japan, for example, GDP rose by 25 per cent between 1976 and 1981, but primary energy consumption rose by less than 3 per cent, and oil consumption fell by 10 per cent.[6]

These are remarkable figures, and a dramatic illustration of the way that changes in relative prices lead to a reallocation of resources—one of the points so much stressed by economists in the course of the growth debate of the early 1970s. Nevertheless, they should not be allowed to induce complacency. One point worth noticing is that the world recession of the early 1980s had, as is often the case, a disproportionate effect on industrial production. Whereas GDP in the twenty-four OECD countries was about $2\frac{1}{2}$ per cent higher in 1981 than it had been in 1979, industrial production hardly rose at all over these two years; and because industrial production is more energy-intensive than other kinds of output, the fall in the ratio of energy consumption to GDP is partly accounted for by this—probably temporary—fall in the ratio of industrial production to GDP. A more fundamental point is that the easiest economies in energy consumption will obviously have been made first; further economies are likely to become progressively more difficult.

There was much talk of an 'oil glut' in late 1981 and 1982, as the factors just described, combined with heavy de-stocking by oil consumers, led to a big fall in the demand for oil, particularly oil supplied by the OPEC countries. OPEC responded to these pressures not by cutting the $34 a barrel reference price but by cutting back production: throughout much of 1982 output was running at well below 20 million barrels a day, compared with about 30 m.b.d. in the later 1970s. Even so, by late 1982 a number of OPEC countries were selling at large discounts on the published price, and spot prices were $30 a barrel or less; and early in 1983 these downward pressures on spot prices were legitimised by a cut in the reference price to $29. This weakness of oil prices, in spite of massive production cutbacks, prompted some governments and companies to talk and act as though the oil crisis was a thing of the past. The rate of oil and gas drilling fell, and a whole series of projects to produce synthetic fuels was scrapped. Exxon—the world's largest oil company—abandoned a huge project to produce oil from shale in Colorado; an even bigger project to derive oil from the Alberta tar sands in Canada was cancelled; and in Britain, BP withdrew from an agreement with the National Coal Board to develop a new kind of coal liquefaction plant. More generally governments, particularly in Britain and America, reduced their support for research and development of new energy sources. Rising capital costs for synthetic fuel plants and very high interest rates played a part in all these decisions, but the major factor was undoubtedly the fall in world oil consumption after 1979, and the widespread belief fostered by this that the real price of oil would be stable or even falling for the rest of the decade.[7]

The attitudes underlying these decisions are likely to prove short-sighted. What happens to oil prices and oil supplies over the next decade or two will both help to determine, and be determined by, the extent of future conservation, and the rate of world economic growth. Views differ markedly. One oil economist has predicted that oil prices may collapse in the late 1980s, and that oil production could go on rising until the middle of the 21st century.[8] A very different view has been taken by a former US Secretary for Energy (Dr James Schlesinger), who said in 1981 that the prospects for future oil supplies were far bleaker than they had been five years earlier, and that 'we are likely to experience another crunch in the middle of the decade unless we work more vigorously on corrective measures'.[9] Two major studies have produced findings which seem closer to the latter position. According to the 'High Scenario' investigated in the IIASA report,[10] under which world GDP would rise by 3.4 per cent a year between 1975 and 2030 (compared with a 5 per cent growth rate between 1950 and 1975) known reserves of conventional oil would be almost exhausted by 2010—in about twenty-five years' time. Even allowing for discoveries of significant new reserves (new North Seas and Mexicos) this outcome would only be postponed for another twenty years.[11] Another authoritative study suggests an even more pessimistic outlook: that world crude oil production may reach a peak as early as 1990, and decline quite rapidly thereafter.[12] On any but the most optimistic assumptions, therefore, it would seem that the contribution of oil—which accounted for nearly 45 per cent of world primary energy consumption in 1980—will be falling fast within the next two or three decades. This raises the question of what is going to replace it.

*

As far as the *generation* of sufficient energy is concerned, there is, physically, no insuperable problem. When oil from conventional sources begins to run out, very large recoverable deposits of natural gas will remain: gas production, already increasing, is unlikely to peak until early in the 21st century, at a level which could then be sustained for several decades, though the problem of transporting large quantities of gas over long distances is still a formidable one. Economically recoverable coal reserves are very large, amounting to perhaps 600 billion tons of coal equivalent, seventy times the amount of *all* primary energy fuels used globally in 1975. Coal *resources* (i.e. deposits that are known or guessed at, though recoverable only at increasing cost) are even vaster —twenty times greater than economically recoverable reserves at a conservative estimate. In addition to coal, there are unconventional oil resources which may amount in total to as much as the world's coal resources: heavy crude oil and tar sands of perhaps 300 billion tons, and oil shale resources which are even greater. Although only 5 or 10 per cent of these unconventional oil resources are recoverable by existing techniques, it seems highly likely that this proportion will be increased by improved technology, if real energy prices continue to rise.

Beyond coal and unconventional oil resources lies nuclear energy. Most existing nuclear power stations are based on 'burner' reactors, which are very inefficient users of the world's limited stocks of natural uranium. But there is another kind of nuclear reactor —the 'breeder' reactor, which uses fissile atoms as a catalyst and not as a fuel, and can therefore, in principle, convert a limited amount of uranium into an unlimited supply of electric power. Although breeder reactors are still in a relatively early stage of development, the technique already exists: a number of breeders are already in operation in different parts of the world, and more are under construction. There seems little doubt that, using breeder technology, energy can be generated in virtually unlimited quantities.

The energy problem, therefore, is not a problem of being unable, in a physical sense, to provide the amount of energy that the world requires. It is clear that with *existing* techniques sufficient energy can be generated for hundreds or thousands of years, if not indefinitely. Existing techniques, too, can in principle supply the answer to another aspect of the energy problem. The easiest energy to supply—though in each case there are transportation problems—will take the form of natural gas, coal, or nuclear-generated electricity. Much of the demand for energy, on the other hand, will continue to be for liquid fuel, such as diesel oil and petrol, both because of the ease with which it can be stored and transported and, more generally, because of the characteristics of the road and air transport, and agricultural, technologies that have been constructed on the basis of more than half a century of cheap oil. This problem can be solved by using coal as a basis for producing synthetic liquid fuels —in effect, converting coal into oil. So-called 'autothermal' techniques of coal liquefaction are already in use, notably in the Sasol plants in South Africa, but are inefficient, losing about half the energy content of the original coal in the process of turning it into oil. However a much more efficient 'allothermal' process has also been developed which, given a sufficient supply of heat generated by nuclear reactors, would permit adequate quantities of liquid fuels to be produced from coal for a century or more into the future.

Existing techniques, then, promise an unlimited supply of energy in the future. They even promise a century or more of the liquid fuels required by the particular technology that has developed on the basis of the cheapness of these fuels in the past. When one takes account of the kind of future technical progress, in both the production and consumption of energy, that all past experience would lead one to expect, it is hard to see why anyone should believe in the existence of an energy problem —however low the social discount rate it seemed appropriate to adopt. Nevertheless, there is a problem, and it is to be found on the other side of the ledger. It lies not in the depletion of exhaustible resources as such, but in the pollution which attends the extraction or use of these resources. This does not appear to include thermal pollution —the amount of waste heat released into the atmosphere —about which some people are worried: the conclusion of a number of studies is that 'waste heat is a nonproblem on the global scale'.[13] It does, however, include pollution of two particularly important kinds.

Natural gas is one of the cleaner fuels: neither its production nor its use give rise to pollution of great significance. Next to natural gas is oil from conventional sources. The last decade has, of course, witnessed some spectacular examples of pollution resulting from accidents in the extraction of crude oil by offshore drilling rigs and the wrecking of supertankers. But the main effects of these oil spills are geographically localised and, so far as is known, relatively short-lived. More serious, from a longer-term point of view, is the emission of sulphur dioxide and carbon dioxide from oil-fired power stations. However, techniques have been devised to reduce the emission of sulphur dioxide, and in any case oil will be increasingly regarded as too precious a commodity to burn in power stations, and be used more and more as a petro-chemical feedstock.

Unfortunately, it is these two relatively clean fuels which are in shortest supply. As was stated earlier, production of natural gas, though certain to make a major contribution to world energy needs over the next few decades, is likely to reach its maximum level within the next thirty or forty years. Oil production from conventional sources will probably peak much sooner. There will be a gradual transition from the era of clean fossil fuels to an era of dirty fossil fuels. The pollution problems arising from this transition will be severe.

Increased reliance on coal as either a direct or indirect energy source is likely to be attended by two problems. The first is the sheer scale of the destruction of life and landscape that may be involved if sufficient quantities of coal are to be mined. Coal mining is a dangerous occupation, and even if future technical progress were to reduce the risks of death, injury or illness to those who work in it, is likely to remain so. Moreover, many of the richest and most accessible seams have already been mined, and although the lack of incentive to discover new coal deposits in recent decades may well mean that vast new deposits await exploitation in, for example, Africa and Asia, the scale of this is uncertain. As time goes on it is clear that — as is already happening in Germany and the western United States — increasingly low-grade deposits will need to be exploited, often by strip-mining techniques, with correspondingly greater destruction of agricultural land or areas of natural beauty.

The second problem is much more intractable, and cannot be shrugged off even by those who may be indifferent to the first. When coal (or any other fossil fuel) is burnt, it releases carbon dioxide into the atmosphere; and once in the atmosphere, there appears to be no way of removing it. The

concentration of carbon dioxide in the atmosphere is thought
to have risen by about 15 per cent over the past century; about
a third of this increase has occurred during the past twenty
years.[14] Not all of this increase has been the result of burning
fossil fuels: a considerable part is probably the result of
deforestation, which reduces the earth's ability to absorb
atmospheric carbon dioxide. But not much comfort can be
drawn from this, since on present trends deforestation will
continue at a rapid rate.[15] There are too many uncertainties to
permit any confident predictions about the effects on atmospheric carbon dioxide of a global energy strategy that is heavily
dependent on coal. To take one example, if the allothermal
techniques of coal liquefaction or gasification referred to
earlier were employed, the release of carbon dioxide for a given
amount of energy generation would be considerably smaller
than if autothermal techniques were employed. Nevertheless,
there seems to be a wide measure of agreement that if present
trends continue the carbon dioxide content of the atmosphere
might have doubled by the year 2050, if not earlier; and a
century later might have doubled, or even quadrupled, again.[16]

   The impact on the world's climate, via the greenhouse effect,
of even a doubling of the carbon dioxide in the atmosphere
would probably be very serious. Calculations suggest that it
would lead to a rise in average global temperature of perhaps 4
centigrade — less in the middle latitudes but considerably more
(perhaps as much as $7-10°$) in the polar regions.[17] This in turn
could lead to the melting of the polar ice caps, and the
consequent flooding of most of the world's coastlines and
many of its major cities. It would also have effects on world
food production which, though impossible to predict, might be
disastrous. And these effects — if they have occurred by the year
2050 — would be felt not only by future generations with which
it may be hard to feel much affinity, but by hundreds of millions
of people who have already been born.

   Thus it is difficult not to regard as unacceptable a longer-
term global energy strategy which is increasingly dominated by
the use of coal. But what is true of coal is also true of
unconventional oil resources: increasing long-term reliance on
heavy crude oil, tar sands or oil shale deposits, apart from

producing a number of other major environmental problems, would lead to the same kind of build-up of carbon dioxide in the atmosphere as increasing reliance on coal. This is by no means to deny the probable need to rely heavily on these resources as a base for synthetic liquid fuels during the next few decades, as conventional oil production peaks and then begins to decline. But a responsible global energy strategy that tries to look fifty or sixty years ahead cannot place any more faith in unconventional oil resources than in coal itself.

This leaves—as far as existing technologies are concerned—nuclear energy. Breeder reactors, as was indicated earlier, can produce virtually unlimited supplies of energy. This would not be a complete answer to the world energy problem, since breeders would make no direct contribution to supplies of liquid fuel. Nevertheless, they would permit large-scale coal liquefaction by allothermal techniques, and in the longer run could make an increasing contribution to road transport as electrically-powered vehicle technology improves.[18] (Nuclear energy is already used directly, of course, to power ships and submarines.)

The problem is that nuclear power is hideously dangerous. This is true of conventional 'burner' reactors, and even more true of breeders. The most dramatic danger, in a conventional nuclear power station, is that a series of accidents will lead to a meltdown of the core: this is what came within an ace of happening at the Three Mile Island plant in Pennsylvania in 1979. The result could be a massive release of radiation which might well kill tens of thousands of people and cause untold long-term genetic damage. Equally dramatic things can happen in a breeder reactor, where the fuel rods need to be bathed not in water but in molten sodium. The slightest leakage of this element into either air or water can provoke a violent explosion. There is evidence that this did in fact happen in a breeder reactor in the USSR in January 1974.[19]

Even more worrying than such accidents, however, are the problems associated with the so-called 'back end' of the nuclear fuel cycle. The spent fuel from nuclear reactors needs to be reprocessed, and one consequence of this activity is the accumulation of quantities of highly radioactive waste—quantities which would, with increasing reliance on nuclear energy, become large. This waste must be stored with absolute security for tens of thousands of years. (Here, too, there appears to be an ominous Russian precedent: an explosion in a nuclear waste dump in 1957 is said to have caused thousands of deaths from radiation sickness and rendered a large part of the Southern Urals uninhabitable.)[20] Yet, despite science-fiction scenarios for solidifying this nuclear waste and shooting it by rocket into the sun, no solution to this problem has been found—nor indeed is readily imaginable. However, the biggest problem of all may lie not in the disposal of radioactive wastes, but in handling the uranium^{-235} and plutonium which are separated out in the reprocessing operation. This applies particularly to the plutonium: the reason why breeder reactors are even more of a threat than burner reactors is that whereas the latter, in effect, involve a uranium-recycling system, the former involve a plutonium-recycling system.

Plutonium is far more toxic than uranium, and probably the most dangerous radioactive material of all. Extraordinarily small deposits of it in the body can cause cancer. Hundreds of millions of pounds of plutonium would eventually be circulating if the breeder reactor was to become the main answer to the world's energy problems.[21] And the half-life of plutonium is 24,000 years. In these circumstances it is difficult to believe that there would not eventually be a build-up of plutonium in the environment—either accidentally or as a result of deliberate terrorist or other action—on a scale that would threaten the very existence of life on the planet. Quite apart from this, the move to a plutonium economy would much increase the danger of proliferation of nuclear weapons, and the prospects of nuclear war. One authority has observed that 'plutonium can be made into a devastating bomb by one or a few people working with material available from a hardware store and an ordinary laboratory-supply house'.[22] No doubt this is an exaggeration; but not enough of an exaggeration for comfort.

11 Energy and the Environment: A Long-term Perspective

The conclusion of the previous chapter can be briefly stated: although existing resources and technologies can generate as much energy as the world is ever going to need, they can almost certainly do so only at a cost which few reflective people would be willing to accept. This unacceptable cost, it must be stressed, is not in any meaningful sense an *economic* cost: it has nothing to do with a rise in the *price* of energy. The real price of energy is likely to rise over the next few decades, as the transition is made from fuels like natural gas and oil, which are relatively cheap to produce and (in the case of oil) to distribute, to those — derived from coal, unconventional oil resources, or nuclear power — which are more expensive. This rising real energy price will lead to all the substitution and conservation measures which economists stress, and which were mentioned earlier: businesses will switch into less energy-intensive products and processes, car engines will become more fuel-efficient, households will install more double-glazing, individuals will take to bicycles, and so on. But the increasingly unacceptable costs of the kind discussed above will *not* be taken account of in this decision-making. The fact that a gallon of petrol or a kilowatt-hour of electricity is being produced by a technique that throws carbon dioxide into the atmosphere or creates a tiny but nonzero risk of releasing plutonium into the environment is not something that affects the price of the petrol or electricity to the individual business or consumer. He will therefore take no account of it in his decision-making.

We are thus faced, once again, by a kind of divergence between private and social costs: the cost to the consumer of using a unit of energy does not fully reflect the cost of its use to society—in this case world society—as a whole. But it is not a divergence that can be eliminated by a system of taxes, subsidies or regulations, in the way that, for example, the costs imposed on society by a firm that discharges noxious chemicals into a river can be internalised, and hence made to impinge on the firm's decision-making, by a suitable tax. The costs—or rather the risks—involved are much too large for that. If, in spite of an increase in its real price, energy demand rises at a rate which can only be met by a big increase in the burning of fossil fuels or the building of hundreds of breeder reactors, then—according to the argument set out above—it will be rising too fast. If appalling dangers are not to gather increasingly over the heads of our children and grandchildren, the consumption of energy must be curbed, or energy must be generated in other ways.

The doomsday scenarios of the early 1970s discussed in Chapter 9 led many people to demand an end to economic growth.[1] In some circles in the United States particularly, a willingness to subscribe to the slogan 'Zero Economic Growth—ZEG' became a touchstone of intellectual seriousness. But stopping economic growth is not an answer to the energy problem. In the first place, it would not stop the build-up of carbon dioxide in the atmosphere, or the spread of breeder reactors, but merely slow these processes down. The threats now facing our grandchildren would be postponed, and face our great-grandchildren instead. That would be an answer of sorts, but not a very satisfactory one. Secondly, and more practically, economic growth is simply not going to stop. Thousands of millions of people in developing countries are not going to be willing to forgo such modest improvements in their low standard of living as may be made possible in the near future by economic growth because of fear of the ecological disaster in the more distant future which is threatened by such growth. This might not matter if people in the industrialised West were willing to accept a steady decline in their own living standards, increasingly forgoing their own consumption of energy so that more could be consumed by developing countries without world consumption as a whole increasing. But that is not going to happen either. To propose that the problem be solved by stopping economic growth is to refuse to face up to the problem.

A second possibility lies in redirecting growth into less energy-intensive channels. To a considerable extent this is happening already as a response to the rise in real energy prices over the past decade, as is illustrated by the boom in such consumer electronics as video tape-recorders and computerised games—products which, in relation to their market value, are economical of energy both to manufacture and to use. No doubt, if real energy prices continue to rise, this trend will continue as well. But if, as was argued above, the rising cost of energy to the consumer fails fully to reflect the increasing risks of greater energy use to the world as a whole, it will not be enough to rely on market forces to redirect economic growth in an appropriate way. At the very least, governments will have to take action as well, by taxing or regulating activities which are heavy consumers of energy, and subsidising or otherwise encouraging activities which are economical in their use of energy. But, as was suggested earlier, the scale on which this can be done is unlikely to measure up to the scale of the problem. Indeed it may be difficult to do on any substantial scale at all. In the West, people may be reluctant to substitute for their cars or their charter flights to holiday resorts such energy-economical activities as walking or reading or knitting. And in developing countries any meaningful rise in living standards is bound to involve rising use of energy: people do not want to spend more time walking ten miles for water, or even meditating under banyan trees, but less. Thus redirecting economic growth in ways that conserve energy can be no more than part of the answer. Much of the answer must lie in a third possibility—developing new sources of energy which are free of the perils posed by fossil fuels and breeder reactors.

There is a variety of inexhaustible or renewable sources of energy. Technologies for harnessing them are at different stages of development, and they differ widely in the extent to which they could contribute to solving the global energy problem. The technology of *hydroelectric* power, for example, is very fully developed. A number of countries, such as Egypt and Ghana, derive most of their electricity from hydroelectric sources, and more could in principle come to do so: rivers originating in the Himalayas, for instance, are virtually untapped. Nevertheless—even if the adverse ecological consequences of such huge projects as Egypt's Aswan High Dam give no pause to future planners in other countries—it is clear that even in the long run hydroelectric power could contribute no more than a small fraction—5 per cent or so—of the energy needed by the world as a whole. *Wind power*—used locally for many years to pump water or generate electricity—has its supporters, who talk of huge windmill farms harvesting great quantitites of energy in the simplest and cleanest of ways. But vast tracts of land would be needed for any significant quantity of output, as well as large amounts of construction materials. Of its nature, wind power would supply a highly variable amount of energy; and of their nature windmill farms would often generate electricity a long way from where it was needed. The well-known difficulties of storing and transporting electricity, in short, would work against it.

Some of the same, as well as other, difficulties apply to the prospects of harnessing the power of the sea. France has been deriving power from the ebb and flow of the tide in the La Rance estuary for more than fifteen years now, but the number of sites suitable for capturing *tidal power* is comparatively limited, and on a global scale its potential contribution is minute. In Britain and a few other island countries *wave power* may come to make a significant contribution, but so far the problem of devising techniques that can cope with great variations in the size of the waves in different weather conditions does not appear to have been overcome. Much more speculative—still no more than a gleam in the eye of the enthusiasts—is 'ocean thermal energy conversion', or OTEC (not to be confused with OPEC)—a technique that would tap solar energy absorbed by the oceans in the equatorial zone as the heat flows, in the form of such ocean currents as the Gulf Stream, towards the polar regions. In a theoretical sense the power that could be tapped in this way is vast—though there would probably be very severe climatic effects. In practice, it seems highly unlikely that any significant amount of energy will be supplied from this source, at any rate for a very long time into the future.

If not the sea, what about the land? *Geothermal* resources are very large: it has been estimated that the total heat stored within the top few miles of the earth's crust at temperatures above 200° centigrade is much greater than the energy content of all the world's fossil fuel resources.[2] But little reliance can be placed on this resource, at any rate during the next fifty years or so: no technology for exploiting it on any significant scale has yet been devised, and there is no way of knowing when such a technology may be developed or how much of the resource could ultimately be used. Another land-based resource is *biomass*—exploiting the solar energy captured by plants or tree leaves. This is already happening on a small scale in a number of countries: in Brazil, for example, ethyl alcohol is being extracted from sugar cane, and there are ambitious plans to expand this activity far enough to make the country entirely self-sufficient in terms of fuel for road vehicles.[3] More generally, biotechnology offers the prospect of generating hydrogen as a by-product of photosynthesis; such hydrogen would have the great advantage as a fuel not only of being easily storable and transportable in either liquid or gaseous form, but of being very clean. Unfortunately, there are strict limits to how far the energy problem can be solved by the exploitation of biomass: quite apart from the ecological risks of the reliance it would involve on fast-growing monocultures, the amounts of land, water and fertilisers that would be needed if biomass was to make a major contribution would be very large indeed, and would add massively to the difficulties the world is going to have anyway in feeding itself.

This brings us to what may turn out to be the answer—but only a long way ahead: *solar energy*. Local (or 'soft') solar energy is already being quite widely used for water and space heating (and, more rarely, air-conditioning) in housing and office blocks. Such usage will certainly spread, and will eventually make a valuable contribution. Nevertheless, measured against global energy demands, the contribution will be a limited one. Much more significant, in the long run, is centralised (or 'hard') solar energy, which promises virtually unlimited supplies of pollution-free energy. Unfortunately, the long run is likely to be very long. A technology already exists for generating electricity from solar energy: large numbers of mirrors reflect sunlight on to a boiler that generates steam. This technology, particularly if improved, could eventually generate electricity on a very large scale; but quite colossal amounts of building materials, particularly steel and concrete, would be required to construct the required number of mirrors, and such a building programme would need many decades to plan and execute. A more promising possibility is the direct conversion of solar energy into electricity by means of photovoltaic cells—a technique already used by spacecraft and communication satellites, but at present very expensive. This might eventually be done by solar satellite power stations—huge solar collectors out in space. But any large-scale contribution to the world energy problem looks a very long way off. It has been reckoned that it will still be negligible, even in fifty years' time.[4]

The same very long time-horizons apply to the other technology which promises unlimited, and clean, energy: *nuclear fusion*. Although in theory this could generate sufficient amounts of electricity or hydrogen to satisfy all conceivable needs, its technological feasibility is not yet established, and perhaps never will be. But even if it is, it is difficult to believe that nuclear fusion could be making much of a contribution to global energy supplies much before the middle of the 21st century.[5]

The position might therefore be summarised as follows. In the long run (perhaps in the second half of the 21st century or beyond) there may well turn out to be no global energy problem. But in this case the long run is—even more than usually—of no more than academic interest. Over the next fifty or sixty years it seems likely that rising demand for energy (even allowing for the fact that rising demand will be held back by rising real energy prices) will only be met, given present policies and priorities, by massively increased reliance on either breeder reactors, or technologies which burn increasingly dirty fossil fuels, or both. The dangers inherent in either of these methods of providing the necessary amounts of energy might reasonably be regarded as unacceptable. But the pressures throughout the world for higher living standards will make it impossible to avoid taking one or both of these highly dangerous routes, whatever warnings dispassionate observers may. issue, unless there is some other way out. And only two possible ways out come to mind. One is a drastic programme of conservation. The other is an accelerated programme of development of inexhaustible and renewable energy sources.

The scale of the problem can be indicated by reference to the findings of the IIASA report (see Chapter 10, note 1). This report considered a number of scenarios for the growth of energy consumption and production up to the year 2030, but for present purposes it is sufficient to look at the 'low' scenario—one in which the demand for energy in 2030 is relatively low. According to this scenario, world GDP grows by 2.4 per cent a year between 1975 and 2030—less than half the 5.0 per cent rate achieved during the quarter century between 1950 and 1975. Given—to take a conventional if pessimistic assumption—a doubling of world population between 1975 and 2030, this would mean an increase in world per capita GDP over this 55-year period of a little over 1 per cent a year. This is not a particularly enthralling prospect but—depending perhaps on how the rise in per capita income was distributed between richer and poorer parts of the world—one which might be regarded as tolerable. On the assumption that energy intensiveness—the ratio of final energy use to GDP—continues to fall in developed countries in line with the historical trend, and that in developing countries, which are building up their industrial base, it initially increases, and then flattens out and eventually starts to decline, then the low scenario yields a total global demand for primary energy in 2030 of 22.4 TW yr/yr, compared with 8.2 TW yr/yr in 1975.[6] This energy demand could be met. But it would be met, in the IIASA scenario, only by heavy reliance on coal (as a source of synthetic liquid fuels) and fast breeder reactors: of the 22.4 TW yr/yr total, 3.3 would come from the fast breeders (and another 1.9 from light water nuclear reactors), and 6.5

from coal (usage of coal being almost three times as high as it was in 1975).[7] On the basis of these calculations it would seem, then, that a rate of growth of world GDP per head of little more than 1 per cent a year is likely to entail very heavy reliance on breeder reactors and coal by 2030: indeed in that year these two sources will between them be providing more energy than was provided by *all* energy sources in 1975.

If, for the sake of illustration, one eliminated from the calculation the contribution from fast breeders (though retaining that from light water reactors) and halved the contribution made by coal, one would have a global primary energy supply figure of approximately 16 TW yr/yr in 2030. As it happens, the IIASA report also briefly considered the implications of keeping energy demand down to this figure. It would not necessarily involve a slower rate of growth of world GDP than the 2.4 per cent projected in the low scenario case, but—on the assumption of a doubling of world population—it would mean no increase at all in per capita energy consumption. In developed economies this would require a substantial shift away from industry, and particularly energy-intensive industry, towards services. Moreover, 'extreme energy-saving measures would have to be introduced in almost every sphere of human activity relating to energy, mandating a radical change in lifestyles of the peoples of all regions' (p. 172). So perhaps, if sufficiently stringent energy-conservation strategies were adopted, demand in 2030 could be kept down to 16 TW yr/yr. But—on the above assumptions—3.25 of this would be supplied by coal and 1.9 of this by burner reactors. The contribution of coal would thus have gradually increased over a 55-year period to a level about half as high again as in 1975; the contribution of nuclear power would have grown until, in 2030, it was fifteen times higher than in 1975. The risks involved in this course of events would undoubtedly be less than those involved in IIASA's low scenario case (22.4 TW yr/yr, of which 6.5 coal and 5.2 total nuclear), let alone its high scenario case (35.7 TW yr/yr, of which 12.0 coal and 8.1 total nuclear); but it can be argued that they are unacceptable nonetheless.

*

We have thus arrived at an unpalatable conclusion. Only if very drastic steps are taken to conserve energy, over and above the effects that will occur anyway as a result of rising real energy prices, does it seem likely that the growth in energy demand will be kept so low that, in fifty years' time, no more than a third of it will be met by (non-breeder) nuclear reactors and coal. Even this scenario means a gradual increase in the use of coal, and hence a significant further increase in the concentration of carbon dioxide in the atmosphere; and a 15-fold increase in the generation of nuclear power, with all the additional risks that such a development would entail.

One way of responding to this prospect is to close one's eyes and hope it will all go away. Maybe safe ways will be devised of reprocessing spent nuclear fuel and disposing of radioactive waste. Maybe the build-up of carbon dioxide in the atmosphere does not matter, or its effects will be offset by something else. Maybe clean and renewable energy resources will be developed sooner than anyone now expects. Maybe the figures are all wrong. Maybe something will turn up.

This is a very natural reaction; it is indeed the way that the world has so far reacted. But it is not a responsible reaction, at any rate for governments which are, or should be, concerned about the welfare of—never mind future generations—millions of existing children who might reasonably expect still to be alive in fifty or sixty years' time. Governments ought to be taking action now in order to reduce the risks that these citizens, and those yet to be born, will face between now and the middle of next century.

The kind of action that governments should be taking is, at least in outline, clear. The world-wide social costs of rising consumption of energy which is generated by coal or nuclear power are greater than the private costs. Governments should therefore be requiring *more* energy conservation and *more* research and development on renewable energy sources than would occur simply in response to rising real energy prices. To this end they should be employing systems of taxes and subsidies, and themselves engaging in expenditure on research and development, on a very much larger scale than at present.

The form which such efforts should take will not be discussed in any detail here, but one or two points may be worth emphasising. It is clear that in the United States in particular, which accounts for more than a quarter of the primary energy consumption of the entire world, there is still a great deal of scope for conservation. Because it developed on the back of apparently unlimited supplies of cheap energy, the US is extremely wasteful in its use of energy: it has been calculated that current lifestyles could be more or less maintained with only half the energy now used; and the other—wasted—half is more than is used by the world's poorest 2 billion people.[8] Rising petrol prices have already had a significant effect on the size of cars Americans buy, and Federal regulations on space heating and cooling standards mean that American offices—though not yet American homes—are no longer furnace-hot in winter and freezing cold in summer. Nevertheless, there is a long way to go. It is particularly important that intensive efforts be made to conserve oil. As was argued earlier, it is world oil production which will peak first; yet oil is of crucial importance for personal transport, as a feedstock for petrochemical manufacture and—because it is so easily transported and stored—for the development of the poorer countries.

Conservation, however, is only part of the story: indeed, as was indicated above, the illustrative figure of energy consumption of 16 TW yr/yr in 2030, which could only be generated, on present trends, by relying very heavily on coal and nuclear power, itself assumes that drastic steps would be taken to conserve energy. Crucial to an energy strategy which does not lead to unacceptable dangers is an accelerated programme of research into, and development of, clean sources of renewable energy. For two reasons, such a programme can only be financed by governments or international organisations. One general reason was mentioned earlier: private agents cannot be expected to act on the basis of social costs and benefits; that is a job for governments. The other, more particular, reason is that any research and development has many of the elements of a public good, and economic theory has demonstrated that public goods are under-supplied by private agents. The benefits of research which led to a satisfactory technique for exploiting wave power, for example, could not be—and certainly *should* not be—confined to those who had financed the research: they would become available to anyone else in a position to exploit wave power. Private companies, therefore, cannot be relied on, of their own accord, to do an optimal amount of this research; it must be done—or subsidised—by government. Indeed the logic of the argument is that not even any single government can be relied on to do enough of this research, unless there is some kind of international agreement, formal or informal, for particular countries to specialise in particular areas of research and development. Otherwise—an instance of the 'free rider' problem discussed in Chapter 7—there will be a temptation for governments to leave it to other governments to finance the research, hoping to cash in on the benefits without having to incur the costs. This is one aspect of the general problem of international cooperation discussed earlier, and taken up again in Chapter 12. For present purposes, however, it seems clear that the main responsibility for financing enough research and development of new, clean energy sources must lie with governments and not with private agents.

Unfortunately, governments are not discharging this responsibility. They are spending far too little on this kind of research and development; so far from increasing this type of expenditure they have, if anything, been reducing it. In the United States President Reagan, soon after taking office, slashed the Department of Energy's budget for the development of synthetic fuels (and later started to dismantle the Department of Energy itself). He also cut back Federal support for fusion programmes to a level, in 1982–83, 25 per cent below the level in 1976–77.[9] In Britain, one of the early acts of the Thatcher government was to make substantial cuts in grants for home insulation, in spite of evidence that expenditure on home insulation can pay for itself, through lower heating bills, in four or five years; and it withdrew grants for industrial energy-saving schemes altogether. Later on the government announced a cutback in its already very modest expenditure on research and development of alternative energy sources, including solar, wind and wave power.[10] In 1981, according to the International Energy Agency, its twenty-one member governments collectively cut their research and development expenditure on non-nuclear energy and conservation by 4.4 per cent; and early in 1982 the European Commission cut back its programme for part-funding the construction of photovoltaic generators in the ten EEC member states.[11] And so on.

Part of the reason for these perverse actions was no doubt to be found in the weakness of oil prices in the early 1980s, and the sense of complacency over energy supplies which the so-called 'oil glut' of 1982 engendered. But a much more general factor was the economic philosophy of the majority of Western governments, and particularly the governments of Britain and the United States. Cuts in public expenditure which permitted cuts in taxation and government borrowing would in turn lead to less inflation and more growth: this, as has been argued earlier, was the notion underlying the economic policies of both Thatcher and Reagan governments. The idea that anything as airy-fairy as expenditure on research and development of new energy resources might escape public expenditure cuts—or should even be increased—was summarily dismissed. Even more fundamental, perhaps, was the fact that economic policy-making in these and other Western countries had simply failed to adjust to the requirements of the *real* energy problem—not the short-term energy problem represented by the oil shocks of the 1970s, but the long-term energy problem that seems likely to afflict the world in the 1990s and into the 21st century. Just as Western governments' economic policies continue to be formulated without regard to the spatial externalities which characterise the contemporary world so, too, do they continue to be formulated without adequate regard to the degree of temporal externalities which now exist. The extent to which conditions on the earth in future decades are being ineluctably determined by today's actions or lack of actions finds little echo in contemporary economic decision-making: the time-horizons remain as short as ever.

The great enemy of those who advocate action to avert the kind of dangers discussed in this chapter is—as was indicated earlier—uncertainty. It is quite true to say that we simply cannot be sure that no absolutely safe ways will ever be devised of transporting and disposing of radioactive waste; nor can we be sure that increasingly heavy reliance on fossil fuels will eventually produce disastrous climatic changes. Accordingly, there is a great temptation to close one's eyes and hope that everything will somehow turn out all right. Even the IIASA report succumbed in part to this temptation, arguing that 'it seems premature to recommend only energy strategies that actively discourage the use of fossil fuels... A period of five to ten years is needed, and can probably be afforded, for vigorous research to narrow the uncertainties sufficiently, in order to be able to decide whether there should be a major shift away from fossil fuels because of the climatic implications' (p. 111). Elsewhere, the report declines to comment on the acceptability of increasing reliance on nuclear power, arguing that 'we view the problems of nuclear waste handling and proliferation as political issues ... outside our factual frame of reference' (p. 192).

The trouble with this attitude is that in this whole field very long lead times, or braking distances, are involved. To develop hard solar power on an adequate scale, for example, is likely to take many decades after the decision to do so is made; and the carbon dioxide content of the atmosphere is likely to go on rising for many decades after everyone decides that the rise must be stopped.[12] Thus while inertia may point in the direction of doing nothing, at any rate for the time being, prudence dictates that something start to be done at once.

From an economic point of view what needs to be done is relatively simple: governments should adopt, in all their decision-making, a shadow price of energy which is higher—and perhaps increasingly higher as time goes on—than the actual price of energy; and this shadow price of energy should also be made to impinge, as far as income distribution considerations allow, on decision-making in the private sector. This would provide a rationale for much greater government subsidies for research, development and demonstration of renewable and inexhaustible energy resources, and for the development and dissemination of techniques of energy conservation. Funds for the development of wave power which may look a waste of money when electricity can be generated from coal at 3 pence per kilowatt-hour, for example, may look a good investment if such electricity is assumed to cost 10 pence per kilowatt-hour. Subsidies to energy-efficient mass transit systems or private home insulation which may look adequate if oil costs $29 a barrel may look very inadequate if oil is deemed to cost $70 a barrel. At the same time, conservation would be much encouraged if indirect taxes, as well as subsidies, were employed to ensure that decisions by private individuals or organisations were based on the government's adopted shadow price: this would mean an increase in taxes on energy, particularly those forms of energy—such as petrol and diesel fuel—where conservation is particularly urgent.

There are two difficulties about such a programme. One is that it would be unpopular. In effect, the government would be increasing the proportion of the national income invested, whether in the form of spending more on research and development, or on insulating buildings, or subsidising the construction of solar collectors; and an increase in investment, at any given level of national income, means a fall in consumption and hence current living standards. This problem, an inevitable consequence of reducing the social discount rate, has already been discussed, and is reverted to again later on.

The other difficulty arises from the need for action to be collective if it is to be of any real use. It is no good one country going to great lengths to conserve energy or develop renewable energy sources because of fears about nuclear power or carbon dioxide in the atmosphere, if other countries simply carry on as before. All countries—or at least all the major industrial countries which account for most of the world's energy consumption—must act together. On nuclear energy, there is not much point in Britain, for example, forgoing the development of breeder reactors if other countries, such as France, have a policy of constructing breeder reactors at breakneck speed. On the carbon dioxide threat, it would not be enough to get concerted action by all twenty-four OECD countries—difficult though even that would be. The Soviet Union, Eastern Europe and China would have to take action as well: together they account for half the world's coal consumption. The Soviet Union and China, moreover, each has far bigger coal reserves than any other country in the world outside the United States.[13] One may well ask whether it is realistic to imagine that either of these countries is going to refrain from exploiting these reserves to the full because of fears of what may happen to the carbon dioxide content of the atmosphere in fifty or a hundred years' time. Yet if they do not cut down their use of coal, there is not a great deal to be gained by relatively small consumers of coal like Britain or West Germany doing so. This problem, too, is taken up again later.

*

Energy has been the focus of the longer-term issues considered in this chapter because shortages of energy in suitable form look like being the main material constraint on economic growth over the next fifty years, and attempts to ease these constraints by turning increasingly to dirty fossil fuels and nuclear power perhaps represent (after nuclear war) the main long-run threats to man's survival. Nevertheless there are many other issues, less directly related to economic policy, in which temporal externalities are of major importance, and where current decisions need to be taken within the framework of a much longer time-horizon than is customary if the longer-term ecological consequences are not to be severe or even catastrophic.

One such problem, already referred to, is the destruction of forests, particularly tropical rain-forests. It has been estimated that by the year 2000 some 40 per cent of the remaining forest cover in developing countries will have disappeared.[14] Deforestation not only reduces the planet's ability to absorb carbon dioxide, and reduces both the quantity and quality of water supplies,[15] but also threatens the extinction of thousands of plants and vertebrate species. This in turn narrows the genetic base of many of the world's crops and livestock, making them more vulnerable to disease, pests and changes in climate, and thus posing some threat to foodchains and overall ecological stability: four-fifths of the world's food supplies are derived from fewer than two dozen plants and animal species.[16] Another problem which directly threatens food supplies is the loss of cropland and degradation of the soil, due to such factors as urban development, soil erosion and desertification, and the effects on crops of air and water pollution, including the increasing salinity of water supplies. It has been estimated that if present trends continue, more than a third of the world's arable land could be destroyed within the next twenty years.[17]

There are a number of other problems of a similar kind. Emissions of sulphur and nitrogen oxides produced by the burning of fossil fuels has led to the problem of acid rain, which has already killed the fish in many of the lakes of Scandinavia and Canada, and in Europe in particular is beginning to do serious damage to crops, forests and buildings. Emissions of chlorofluorocarbons and some other substances threaten to deplete the ozone layer, which would increase the amount of ultra-violet radiation reaching the surface of the earth and might lead to various adverse effects on plant and animal life, including a rising incidence of skin cancer. More generally, the release into the environment of many of the 70,000 chemicals now in commercial use may have longer-term effects of a kind that no one can now foresee.

These problems vary greatly in the difficulties they present. Action to reduce or prevent depletion of the ozone layer, for example, is readily imaginable: some 90 per cent of both production and consumption of chlorofluorocarbons takes place in OECD countries, and agreement to reduce emissions could probably be fairly easily reached; indeed a number of OECD countries have already taken steps to reduce the use of these substances in aerosols. Action to halt or even significantly slow down the destruction of tropical forests, on the other hand, presents exceedingly formidable difficulties. For the most part these forests lie in developing countries which desperately need the hardwood exports, fuel-wood and new agricultural land provided by the felling of this timber, and which in any case mainly lack the administrative and technical expertise to prevent activities which may have devastating consequences in the long run but which are often highly profitable to private interests in the short run.

From the point of view of macroeconomic policy, however,

all these problems, together with the energy problem discussed at length earlier on, have one thing in common. They can only be solved at the expense of current levels of consumption. If tomorrow's living standards are to be protected, today's must fall, not necessarily in absolute terms, but certainly in relation to what would otherwise be possible. To take a very trivial example: if people in fifty or a hundred years' time are not to suffer the consequences of depletion of the ozone layer, people today will have to do without aerosol hair sprays. To take a more substantial example: if people are to have adequate supplies of safe energy in the future, they must make do with less energy, and pay more taxes to finance research and development of renewable energy sources, in the present. The issue can be looked at in another way—in national income accounting terms. It is customary to deduct 10 per cent or so from a country's gross national product, in order to allow for depreciation or capital consumption, before arriving at the figure for net national product—the amount of a country's net income. A country that consumes more than its net income—i.e. that fails to maintain the level of its capital stock—is storing up trouble for the future. This is precisely what is happening on a global scale. The world as a whole is not investing enough to maintain tolerable conditions in the longer run. It is consuming the environment.

We thus reach this chapter's final conclusion. Macro-economic policy may have been able until now to ignore anything that lies more than a few years ahead; but it must do so no longer. Explicit policies need to be formulated and carried out which will prevent the environment being degraded to such an extent that within a few generations life becomes intolerable or even impossible. But for a large minority of the human race life is already intolerable, or close to it. We must beware of being so concerned not to sacrifice the future to the present that we blithely sacrifice the present to the future. Massive new investment, in the widest sense of the word, is required if in future safe energy supplies are to be forthcoming, and if the world is to be able to feed itself. There is little surplus in the developing countries to finance such investment; it must come from the richer countries of the West, and the Soviet bloc. But even in these countries people will only be willing to save and invest a larger proportion of the GDP—if they are willing at all—if GDP is at the maximum level permitted by technology and the size of the labour force, and growing along the path made possible by technical progress. And this brings us full circle: back to the question of achieving full employment and growth in the 1980s and 1990s.

12 Pulling the Threads Together

The time has come to try to pull together the two main threads which have been running through this analysis—the spatial and the temporal. For any solution to one set of problems must be consistent with—and preferably itself promote—a solution to the other.

The basic spatial problem, it has been argued, arises from the increase in the interdependence of the world economy over the past ten or fifteen years. For most countries, exports and imports represent a significantly larger proportion of GDP than they used to; and much larger sums of capital can and do get moved from one country or currency to another than used to be the case. Yet this growth in the strength and extensiveness of the economic and financial links that bind countries together has not been accompanied by much change in the way that countries formulate economic policies. These policies continue to be determined almost exclusively by the government's perception of the country's domestic needs; little or no thought is given to their likely effects on other countries. In a general way, this habit of ignoring externalities is bound to lead to a suboptimal outcome for the world as a whole. The particular form which this suboptimal outcome seems to take is an unnecessary loss of output and employment. This is influenced by the values and preferences of the world financial community, which favour countries which are pursuing orthodox or conservative fiscal and monetary policies rather than those pursuing expansionary policies, and currencies which are more likely to appreciate than depreciate. Thus countries which—ignoring the effects on the rest of the world—adopt deflationary policies for domestic reasons will tend to find these policies supported and validated by the reactions of the world financial community; and these deflationary policies will have deflationary effects elsewhere. But countries which—also ignoring the effects on the rest of the world—adopt expansionary policies for domestic reasons are likely to be faced by reactions from the world financial community which force these policies to be abandoned; the expansionary effects elsewhere will be minimal. Thus the overall result, in the interdependent world which has developed, of a national decision-making process which largely ignores externalities is a deflationary bias in the working of the international economy.

The temporal problem has two aspects, one relatively short-term and transient, the other long-term and probably permanent. The first of these relates particularly to the technological revolution associated with microelectronics. It seems likely that over the next decade or two there will be a massive gross displacement of jobs in OECD countries as a result of the spread of microelectronic processes, and competition from the newly-industrialising countries. If this is not to result in involuntary long-term unemployment on a huge scale, two responses are probably going to be needed. One is a large programme of training and re-training to equip the labour force with the kind of skills—many of them likely to be exercised in the public sector—which will not be rendered obsolete by microelectronics. The other is a redefinition of the concept of paid employment, such that work, as traditionally defined, will normally account for a significantly smaller proportion of a person's waking hours than it does at the moment. Both these responses will take a considerable time to plan and execute, not only because of the time required to set up training programmes on the necessary scale, but also because of the major shift in attitudes towards work and leisure—and probably towards the role of the public sector— that is going to be needed. The traditional two or three-year time-horizon of macroeconomic policy is not going to be enough. If full employment—even redefined in the way suggested above—is to be achieved in the mid-1990s, for example, it will not be sufficient to adopt a particular macroeconomic stance in the early 1990s: long-term plans will have to be worked out much sooner than that.

The second aspect of the temporal problem looks less immediately threatening than the kind of technological unemployment just referred to: but it also looks inherently less manageable. Just as the last ten or fifteen years have witnessed an increase in spatial interdependence which has partially invalidated the traditional assumptions of macroeconomic policy-making, so also has it seen the growth of a well-founded concern about the longer-term consequences for the environment of the kind of economic growth that it is one of the main objectives of economic policy to promote. Perhaps within a few decades, but certainly by the middle of the 21st century, these problems—deforestation, loss of cropland, and above all the pollution of the atmosphere by the carbon dioxide and radioactivity resulting from the ever increasing generation of energy—will be starting to threaten the continued existence of a large part of—perhaps all of—mankind. Yet this increasing threat finds no recognition in contemporary economic policy-making. Macroeconomic policy is still formulated within much the same time-horizon as it was thirty or forty years ago: the focus is on output and employment and inflation over the next year or two, and the effects on the environment of present or future levels of industrial output simply do not enter into consideration. It may seem visionary or even—given the intractability of our contemporary economic difficulties—irresponsible to demand that today's economic decisions be made with part of an eye on their implications for the world in 2030 or 2035. But the 2030s are no further away from us than the 1930s, and few thoughtful people can be unaware of how far the present political and economic state of the world is the legacy of what happened in the 1930s. And—assuming there is no nuclear holocaust in the meantime—hundreds of millions of people who will be experiencing the 2030s are already alive today.

A possible response to this argument is that the existence of the spatial problem may itself constitute a solution to the temporal problem: that the near-zero growth of world output and trade in the early 1980s, and the apparent prospect of little improvement in the immediate future, mean that the problems of resource depletion and environmental pollution associated with economic growth can safely be ignored. But it is this view which is irresponsible, and indeed naive. It is irresponsible because the continuation of near-zero economic growth would inevitably be accompanied by ever-increasing levels of unemployment and—in a world in which population is increasing by nearly 2 per cent a year—falling living standards for nearly everybody. Quite apart from the colossal waste, misery and indeed mortality this would involve, such an outcome would be bound to produce before long a series of violent social and political upheavals. It is naive because zero economic growth would in any case not solve the problems of resource depletion and environmental pollution discussed earlier in the book, but merely postpone by a decade or two the stage at which they become acute. The plain fact is that if life on the planet is to remain, or become, tolerable—perhaps, indeed, if it is even to remain *possible*—solutions must be found to both the spatial problem and the temporal problem.

Two potential solutions to the spatial problem—the deflationary bias imparted to the world economy by independent and inward-looking decision-making in a highly interdependent world—were canvassed in Chapter 7. One lay in 'de-linking': a deliberate reduction in the extent of interdependence, with individual countries using such measures as import and exchange controls to lessen the vulnerability of their own key economic variables to decisions and developments in other countries, and to the views of the world financial community. The other lay in a markedly greater degree of coordination of economic policies among the main OECD countries, so that individual countries were forced to take explicit account of the effects of their policies on other countries, and encouraged to adopt reasonably expansionary policies in exchange for the pledge that such policies would also be adopted by others. Although the tenor of the argument in that chapter was that the disadvantages of de-linking might be greater than the disadvantages of co-ordination, particularly in

the short run, a certain degree of agnosticism seemed appropriate in drawing conclusions.

No corresponding agnosticism is sustainable in the case of
the temporal problem. Of its very nature, the temporal
problem—the radiation risks of nuclear power, the climatic
effects of deforestation and the build-up of carbon dioxide in
the atmosphere—is a global problem. No individual country
can de-link itself from this problem. Only global solutions are
conceivable. Such global solutions will require the co-
operation of, at a minimum, most of the OECD and Eastern
European countries, the Soviet Union and China.

The fact that the long-term temporal problem can only be
solved on the basis of international co-operation has powerful
implications for the best way to approach the spatial problem.
It is highly implausible to suppose that countries which are
turning in upon themselves, deliberately reducing their trading,
financial and other links with each other, are at the same time
going to engage increasingly in the kind of international co-
ordination and regulation that will be required if massive
longer-term damage to the environment is to be avoided. It is
true that the simpler life styles advocated by many of those who
are most concerned about the future of the environment are
fully consistent with de-linking: it is certainly quite easy to
imagine a country in which QOL (quality of life) is regarded as
a more important concept than GDP being one with relatively
limited trading and financial links with the rest of the world.
But it seems unlikely that simpler life styles—even on the
implausible assumption that they were widely adopted
—would by themselves provide an answer to the environmental problems which loom in the longer term. Such life styles
can have negative externalities of a kind that constitute much
of the environmental problem: massive deforestation, for
example, which poses such a threat to the planet's future
climate, is largely the result of attempts by people in developing
countries with exceedingly simple life styles to grow enough
food and gather enough firewood to stay alive. This is not to
deny that the adoption of simpler life styles in the West—more
reliance on bicycles and less on cars, to take a trite
example—may not make a useful, conceivably even essential,
contribution towards coping with the energy problem. But

such a change in life styles would still need to take place in the context of increased international policy co-ordination if the longer-term environmental problems are going to be effectively tackled.

However, although international co-operation is essential if these longer-term environmental problems are to be solved, since it is no good one or two countries taking action if others fail to do so, a prior condition of such co-operation is that individual governments should be persuaded of the need for action. And the action required, as was discussed in Chapter 11, will involve a reduction—or at any rate a slower growth—in living standards, as a larger proportion of the GDP is invested in energy conservation, research and development of alternative energy sources, and in other ways.

The difficulty of getting governments to take this problem seriously can hardly be overestimated. Countries in which there is most likely to arise a body of enlightened opinion willing and able to bring pressure to bear on governments on this issue are, almost by definition, the more democratic countries. But it is in precisely these countries that governments, faced by the need to seek re-election every few years, and having to contend with the promises of parties in opposition, are under most pressure to produce satisfactions in the present, and to ignore problems that may not become apparent for twenty years or more into the future. A hopeful sign in this context is the emergence in a number of Western European countries—particularly Germany, and to a lesser extent France—of ecological or 'green' parties which are concerned about environmental problems. Although as yet numerically small—and covering a wide spectrum of often bizarre opinion—they could in some circumstances come to hold the balance of power between the conventional left and right, and influence the formation of policy on environmental issues accordingly. It is at least a beginning.

Another group of countries whose co-operation will be needed if the dangers inherent in the spread of nuclear—particularly breeder—reactors and the build-up of carbon dioxide in the atmosphere are to be significantly reduced comprises the Soviet Union, China and East European countries. These countries are not democracies in the

Western sense, and their governments are for the most part ruthlessly intolerant of internal dissent. This does not, however, mean that their economic policies are formulated within a longer time-perspective than those of the Western democracies. Although these regimes cannot be removed from office at the ballot box, they do have to respond within limits to the contemporary requirements and demands of their own citizens. Being in varying degrees inefficient (one thinks of Soviet agriculture) and needing to spend relatively large sums on maintaining internal security (one thinks of Poland), they have no great surplus left over which they are inclined to devote to the kind of investment needed if environmental problems are to be adequately tackled. In spite of all this, it does not seem utopian to suppose that these countries could be persuaded to co-operate in a global strategy for saving the environment. They all possess sophisticated and rational decision-making processes, and influential scientific elites capable of identifying and emphasising the massive environmental threats that lie only a few decades ahead.

Much more of a problem is posed by the developing countries. Although the threat from the burning of fossil fuels and the spread of breeder reactors in these countries is small compared with that in the advanced industrial countries, it is mainly in the developing countries that other threats, such as deforestation and desertification, are at their most acute. It is not difficult to take a pessimistic view of the prospects for effective action on this front. Many developing countries in Latin America, Africa and even Asia are in the hands of military or semi-military dictators whose concern for the welfare of their existing citizens is so minimal that there is not much point in expecting them to show any concern for future ones. Even in the more enlightened and democratic of the developing countries, the likelihood of appropriate environmental action must be adjudged remote. People struggling on the margin of subsistence, and the governments which represent them, cannot reasonably be expected to worry very much about what may happen in twenty or thirty years' time.* The

---

* Chekhov's Astrov, deploring the destruction of the Russian forests that had taken place in his own lifetime, made the point precisely: 'Here we

only way in which they are likely to be persuaded to take the action needed, for example, to halt or slow down deforestation or the loss of cropland is if they are compensated—or overcompensated—for doing so by other countries. Even in the unlikely event of the Soviet bloc proving much more generous than it has done in the past, what this amounts to is bigger aid budgets in the OECD countries. In other words, at a time when such environmentally responsible policies as Western governments can be persuaded to adopt will already be eating into current living standards, additional resources will be needed to fund the cost of environmentally responsible policies in the developing countries. This is logical enough: the global environment is a seamless web, and it would make little sense for Western governments to agree to spend money in their own countries to promote energy conservation or the development of alternative clean energy sources while at the same time refusing to finance action in developing countries designed to have the same effect and quite possibly yielding a higher return. From another angle, it could be argued that since it is the well-off Western countries that have most to lose from environmental degradation, it is only right that they should shoulder most of the burden of preventing it. Nevertheless, none of this alters the fact that the need to make more resources available to developing countries if environmental problems are to be effectively tackled on a global scale is going to impose even greater demands on the statesmanship of Western governments than the need for action in their own countries alone would indicate.

The fact that massive resources will need to be deployed if looming environmental problems are to be coped with, and that a very large proportion of these resources will need to come from OECD countries, emphasises the critical importance of bringing these countries back to full employment and reasonable rates of growth. It is going to be difficult enough in the most favourable circumstances to persuade people to forgo

have a picture of decay due to an insupportable struggle for existence . . . as when a sick, hungry, shivering man, simply to save what is left of his life and to protect his children, instinctively, unconsciously clutches at anything which will satisfy his hunger and keep him warm, and in doing so destroys everything, without a thought for tomorrow.'[1]

some current consumption in order to invest in solutions to environmental problems that lie decades ahead; it is likely to be quite impossible if current living standards are already depressed by the effects of idle resources and very low rates of growth. For reasons given earlier, a strategy of de-linking—even if such a strategy were capable of restoring full employment and reasonable rates of growth in individual countries—is not likely to be consistent with the kind of extensive international co-operation that will be needed if environmental problems are to be dealt with. The restoration of full employment and growth must be achieved through the international co-ordination of national economic policies.

There are two obstacles in the path to such co-ordination. The first, and immediate, difficulty lies in the monetarist philosophy which has established such a grip on economic policy-making, particularly in Britain and the United States, since the end of the 1970s. According to this philosophy, the economy is basically self-stabilising, and the government should confine its activities to balancing the budget and controlling the growth of the money supply in a way consistent with stable prices. What the government should *not* do is intervene in the economy at the macro level, using its various fiscal, monetary or other instruments to influence the level of demand, and hence the level of output and employment. If one accepts this monetarist philosophy, and rejects the need for discretionary macroeconomic policies, one will *a fortiori* reject the need for international co-ordination of such policies, and there is nothing more to be said.

But the monetarist philosophy is becoming noticeably threadbare, as it becomes increasingly apparent that modern economies do not work in the way postulated by monetarist models. The pursuit of monetarist policies in a number of OECD countries over the past few years, most notably in Britain and the US, has led to a fall in output and rise in unemployment on a much bigger scale than seems to have been anticipated, a process which has been compounded by the deflationary bias in the working of the world economy. Although monetarist economists and commentators in Britain and the US had been predicting an imminent strong economic upturn ever since 1980, there were still few signs of it even two years later. It is hardly surprising that by the autumn of 1982 public opinion in both these countries should have become much more concerned about unemployment than about inflation. In the United States the Federal Reserve Board, under heavy pressure from the Administration and Congress, responded by relaxing its tight control of the money supply. In Britain, on the other hand, Mrs Thatcher stood her ground; but it was ground that remained tenable only because of quite extraneous political circumstances, and even so would not remain tenable for ever.

Thus the increasingly apparent costs of monetarist remedies in terms of lost output and employment, together with the probably transient nature of the fall in inflation which has accompanied their use,[2] hold out some hope that they will soon be discarded, and the philosophy behind them repudiated. This will remove one obstacle to greater international co-ordination of expansionary national policies.

The second obstacle is of longer standing. It lies in the jealously-guarded sovereignty of the nation state. In the foreign policy field individual governments are, by definition, concerned with the actions and reactions of other governments. Economic policy is different: decisions are traditionally taken with a view to their effect on a government's own citizens, and them alone. It is true, as was pointed out in Chapter 2, that these decisions will be taken in the light of expected developments abroad, particularly in an open economy which relies heavily on its exports to other countries. It is also true that for the last thirty or forty years OECD countries have been operating under rules or codes of conduct—such as those laid down by GATT or the IMF—that constrain their freedom of action in various ways. EEC members have been further constrained in the economic measures they can adopt by the provisions of the Treaty of Rome and subsequent Community legislation. In spite of this, the habit is deeply ingrained for governments to think of macroeconomic policy—the very heart of their decision-making processes, and the policy which has the greatest impact on their chances of re-election—as a matter for themselves alone. The notion that macroeconomic decisions should only be made after consultation with—and, up to a point, with the approval of—other governments is one which does not find ready acceptance. Nevertheless, this is what is now called for. The degree of economic and financial interdependence in the world economy is now so great that economic decisions in the major OECD countries, and particularly in the United States, have significant effects on other countries. Elementary welfare economics, and indeed ordinary common sense, require that these external effects be taken into account if these decisions are to lead to the best results. More specifically, unco-ordinated and inward-looking decision-making by the major countries has a net deflationary effect on the world economy, since deflationary policies tend to be validated by the international financial community, while expansionary ones are discouraged. Only a co-ordinated expansion is likely to be successful in pulling the world out of the recession of the early 1980s, and maintaining a reasonable level of employment and rate of economic growth in the future. It is the reluctance of individual governments to recognise the logic of this argument that constitutes the second obstacle to the kind of co-ordinated expansion that is needed.

There is some hope. As long ago as the Bonn summit of the seven main OECD countries in July 1978 an attempt was made to reach mutual agreement on appropriate macroeconomic policies. On that occasion the US, which had been expanding quite rapidly for nearly three years, agreed to adopt various anti-inflationary measures; and, as a crucial contribution towards reducing its oil imports, to raise internal oil prices to the world market level by the end of 1980. Each of the other countries committed itself to taking expansionary action provided the others did likewise. Japan, running a current account surplus of $17 billion in 1978, undertook to limit its exports temporarily and to expand domestic demand so as to increase the rate of growth of total output by $1\frac{1}{2}$ per cent. Germany, running a $9 billion current account surplus, promised action to raise GNP by 1 per cent. France, in a less favourable balance of payments position, promised action to increase its budget deficit by $\frac{1}{2}$ per cent of GNP; Italy and Canada likewise undertook to raise their growth rates; and Britain pointed out that it had only recently given a stimulus to its economy equivalent to rather over 1 per cent of GDP.

It was extremely unfortunate that by the time of the next economic summit, held in Tokyo in late June 1979, the civil war in Iran and the cessation for several months of Iranian oil exports had led to a 50–60 per cent rise in oil prices; and that by the time of the Venice summit of June 1980, oil prices were well over double what they had been two years earlier. The consequence was that at both these summits heads of governments—particularly those of Germany and Japan—were much more concerned with the inflationary and balance of payments effects of the oil price increase than with the need to continue with expansionary policies. As a result, the initiatives taken at the Bonn summit were never properly followed through into a systematic strategy of co-ordinated expansion. Indeed, since the large current account deficits sustained by Germany and Japan in both 1979 and 1980 were the result not only of the oil price increase but also to some extent of the expansionary action they had agreed to take at the Bonn summit, they may subsequently have come to regret these undertakings.

Later summits have not always been a success, and indeed have sometimes seemed to be staged mainly for the benefit of the media. The June 1982 Versailles summit is remembered mainly as having aggravated a long and acrimonious row between the United States and the European countries over economic relations with the Soviet bloc. The Williamsburg summit of May 1983 was chiefly used by President Reagan to secure the support of his major allies for his controversial arms deployment proposals; little progress was made in convincing him of the need for a reduction in the structural American budget deficit in order to reduce world interest rates.

Nevertheless, whatever the deficiencies of recent summits, these occasions—and particularly the kind of agreement reached at Bonn—remain a hopeful portent for the future. The seven countries represented at these periodic summits account between them for about 85 per cent of OECD output, and some 60 per cent of world trade. If they can agree, and continue to agree, on co-ordinated policies of expansion, the rest of the world will be pulled along in their wake, and resources will become available both to raise contemporary living standards and to deal with the environmental problems which loom in the more distant future.

If they cannot agree, the outlook is bleak indeed.

Notes

CHAPTER 2

1   See Phillips, 1958, and Paish and Hennessy, 1964.
2   Matthews, 1968.
3   Dow, 1964.
4   The twenty-four members of the Organisation for Economic
    Co-operation and Development (OECD) are, broadly speaking,
    the democracies of Europe, North America and Australasia, and
    Japan. The seven main member countries—those which attend
    the annual economic Summits—are the US, Canada, Germany,
    France, Britain, Italy and Japan. Together, these seven account
    for about 85 per cent of total OECD output.
5   Hansen, 1969. According to this study, both discretionary
    intervention and automatic stabilisers had worked to stabilise
    the economy in the United States, Germany and Sweden; in
    France and Italy discretionary intervention had been destabilis-
    ing, but this had been more than offset by the operation of
    powerful automatic stabilisers. Only in Britain had both discre-
    tionary intervention and automatic stabilisers been destabilis-
    ing. However, the methodology of the study was criticised by
    some economists (e.g. Kennedy, 1973) and its findings were not
    universally accepted as valid.
6   Jay, 1976.
7   The Federal Reserve Board is 'a creature of Congress,' and
    accepts Congress's right to issue it directives. By the autumn of
    1982 Congress was pressing the FRB to relax its tight monetary
    policies, and at the end of the year took the unusual step of
    issuing instructions to that effect (reported in *Financial Times*, 24
    December 1982).

8   It would not be surprising if the rise in unemployment was much greater than Mrs Thatcher had anticipated. Responding to a questionnaire from the House of Commons Treasury and Civil Service Committee in June 1980, Milton Friedman, by whose economic views Mrs Thatcher had been much influenced, said at one point, 'I conclude that (a) only a modest reduction in output and employment will be a side effect of reducing inflation to single figures by 1982, and (b) the effect on investment and the potential for future growth will be highly favourable' (Memoranda on Monetary Policy, 720, p. 61). In fact, real GDP fell by nearly $2\frac{1}{2}$ per cent in 1980 and by even more in 1981; unemployment, which had been $5\frac{1}{2}$ per cent of the labour force when Mrs Thatcher took office in May 1979, had reached 13 per cent by the autumn of 1982, and was still rising; and by late 1982 manufacturing investment was running at a level about 30 per cent below 1979.

9   If a government's expenditure consisted entirely of the payment of old age pensions, for example, and it financed this expenditure entirely from the yield of a tax on capital gains, the effect would be very expansionary: old age pensions are very largely spent on consumption, whereas capital gains tax probably has little effect in reducing the consumption of those who pay it. At the other extreme, government expenditure consisting entirely of the acquisition of existing assets (nationalisation), but financed entirely by indirect taxes such as value added tax, would have a highly deflationary effect on the economy.

10 In some countries—particularly some developing countries—the government may be promoting the interests of no more than a small ruling clique, or indeed of powerful foreign governments or corporations; but this would not generally be thought true of the main OECD countries with which this book is chiefly concerned.

CHAPTER 3

1   World Bank, *World Development Report 1982*, p. 13.
2   Yearbook of International Trade Statistics, 1980, Vol. I, UN, New York, 1981; and UN Yearbook of National Accounts Statistics, 1980, Vol. II, New York, 1980.
3   Japan's share of world exports of manufactures rose from 9.4 per cent in 1965 to 15.6 per cent in 1978, and had risen to 18.0 per cent in 1981 (*National Institute Economic Review*, August 1975 and November 1982).

4 *National Institute Economic Review*, November 1982, Tables 22 and 23. World exports of manufactures are not, of course, the same as OECD exports, but the two series are fairly closely correlated.

5 World Bank, *World Development Report 1982*, Table 2.7.

6 World Bank, *op. cit.*, Table 4.3.

7 IMF *World Economic Outlook*, 1982, Tables 30 and 31.

8 Thus the debt service ratios (payments as a percentage of exports of goods and services) of non-oil developing countries as a whole had risen from 14 per cent in the mid-1970s to an estimated 22.3 per cent in 1982 (IMF *World Economic Outlook*, 1982, Table 33).

9 The point has been put rather racily by Walter Wriston, Chairman of Citibank: 'If Exxon pays Saudi Arabia fifty million dollars all that happens is that we debit Exxon and we credit Saudi Arabia. The balance of Citibank remains the same. And if they say they don't like American banks, they'll put it in Credit Suisse, all we do is charge Saudi Arabia and credit Credit Suisse: our balance sheet remains the same. So when people run around waiting for the sky to fall there isn't any way that money can leave the system.' (Quoted in Sampson, 1981, p. 141)

10 In 1981, 'the external claims of banks in the Group of Ten countries, Switzerland, Austria, Denmark and Ireland and of branches of US banks in offshore centres of the Caribbean and Far East expanded from $1,322 billion to $1,542 billion'. After eliminating double-counting resulting from the redepositing of funds between reporting banks, the expansion in 1981 was 'roughly $165 billion, or 21.5 per cent, to a total of about $940 billion' (Bank for International Settlements, Fifty-second *Annual Report*, 1981–82, p. 115).

CHAPTER 4

1 This argument rests on the assumption that a major cause of inflation is the response of workers, in the form of higher money wage demands, to a failure of their real wages to rise at a rate they consider acceptable. There is some empirical support for this belief in Britain, though less in other countries (see, for example, Jackson, Turner and Wilkinson, 1972, and recent issues of the Cambridge *Economic Policy Review*).

2 In the extreme monetarist case, in which the money supply is held constant and the demand for money is stable with respect to income and is also zero interest-elastic, increased government expenditure will crowd out private expenditure 100 per cent, so

that there will be no increase in the overall level of activity in the economy. The argument in the text makes the Keynesian assumption that the interest-elasticity of the demand for money is above zero, and that the money supply is not necessarily held completely constant.

3 According to modern portfolio theory, a change in relative interest rates leads to an immediate once-for-all adjustment of portfolios, rather than a continuing flow of capital. In practice, however, various lags in the system usually cause this adjustment to be spread over a period of time. The use in the text of the terms 'influx', 'inflow', 'outflow' etc. is intended to comprehend in a broad way both theory and practice.

4 If the *whole* of the increase in the budget deficit is financed by borrowing from the banking system there is likely to be some *fall* in interest rates as private investors purchase government securities in order to maintain balanced portfolios. The case in the text assumes that a sufficient proportion of the fiscal expansion is financed by sales of gilts to ensure that—given the size of the transactions demand for money and other factors—interest rates are kept constant.

CHAPTER 5

1 See for example Barnet and Muller, 1974.
2 A revealing Chase Manhattan Bank advertisement in the *Financial Times* on 23 September 1982 said: '\$112 billion. That's the amount Chase transfers around the world on an average day.'
3 In practice this simplifying assumption is unlikely to be correct, as different kinds of government expenditure and revenue have different weights in their effect on demand (see Chapter 2, note 9); but this does not affect the basic argument.
4 E. Cary Brown, 'Fiscal Policy in the Thirties: a Reappraisal', *American Economic Review*, December 1956 (and in *National Institute Economic Review*, February 1977, p. 44).
5 *National Institute Economic Review*, February 1982, p. 7 and May 1982, p. 34. The same point can be represented another way. Between 1980–81 and 1981–82 the PSBR, at 1982 prices, was reduced from £15.9 billion to £9.2 billion—clearly a deflationary change. But the total cost to the Exchequer of unemployment, from lower tax receipts and higher social security benefits, rose between these two years from £9.4 billion to £13.9 billion (calculated by Institute for Fiscal Studies, as

reported in *Sunday Times*, 14 November 1982). Thus the total fiscal stance can be said to have been tightened by £4.5 billion *more* than the £6.7 billion reduction in the PSBR would suggest.

6 In 1981, for example, gross private domestic saving represented 32.3 per cent of GNP, whereas private domestic investment represented 25.6 per cent of GNP (IMF *World Economic Outlook*, April 1982, Table 60).

7 Bank for International Settlements, Fifty-first *Annual Report*, 1980–81.

CHAPTER 6

1 The problem was exactly the same, on an international scale, as the one Keynes had analysed on a national scale in the *General Theory*. If, in a national context, *ex-ante* (or intended) saving at full employment exceeds *ex-ante* investment, national income will fall until *ex-post* (or actual) saving and investment are equal. If this fall in national income is to be avoided, the government must take steps to increase *ex-ante* investment or reduce *ex-ante* saving. Similarly, if, on a word scale, *ex-ante* current account surpluses at a high level of income and output exceed *ex-ante* current account deficits, world income and output will fall until *ex-post* surpluses and deficits are equal. Hence — if nothing can be done in the short run about the level of *ex-ante* surpluses — the importance of governments agreeing to accept the required level of *ex-ante* deficits.

2 See McCracken, 1977, pp. 66–80, for a discussion of events at this time.

3 McCracken, 1977, p. 72.

4 Pliatzky, 1982, p. 213.

5 For a well-researched account of how this belief gained ground, and of the events that followed, see Stephen Fay and Hugo Young, 'The day the £ nearly died', *Sunday Times*, 14, 21 and 28 May 1978. See also Pliatzky, 1982, pp. 147–61.

6 The US Treasury Secretary, William Simon, had previously been a Wall Street bond broker. The Treasury Under-Secretary for monetary affairs, Edwin Yeo, came to the job direct from a bank in Pittsburgh. Both men — but particularly Simon — were regarded as conservative even by American standards.

7 This last requirement was actually expressed in terms of a reduction in domestic credit expansion (DCE); as long as the balance of payments on current account remained in deficit the increase in the money supply would have to be smaller than DCE.

8   Pliatzky, 1982, p. 159. See also article by same author in *Financial Times*, 15 March 1982.
9   An aggravating factor is that the United States has a low propensity to save, no tax inducements to saving, and a system of tax relief on interest payments on borrowing. Japan, by contrast, has a high propensity to save, tax inducements to savers, but no tax relief on interest payments by borrowers. (*Financial Times*, 1 April 1982.) The effect of these differences is to push American interest rates up, and Japanese interest rates down, in relation to each other; and hence to increase the inducement to Japanese to lend to America, and Americans to borrow in Japan. Simple textbook theory would predict that arbitrage would eliminate these interest rate differentials. One of the reasons why it does not lies in the offsetting behaviour of *forward* exchange rates (see Llewellyn, 1980).

CHAPTER 7

1   The kind of approach discussed here has been consistently advocated over the years by, among others, the Cambridge Economic Policy Group, as being the only workable solution to Britain's macroeconomic problems. The emphasis here differs somewhat, however, from that of the CEPG, in that the analysis is regarded as applying to any country whose expansion has been inhibited by the deflationary bias inherent in the working of the international economy (and, as was argued in the last chapter, this has been true in recent years of such powerful countries as Germany and the United States), and not just to the special case of Britain. Secondly, the Cambridge group assumes that inflation is mainly the result of wage earners' attempts to secure a steady rise in real wages that is greater than the economy's capacity to deliver, and that this required increase in real wages does not vary much with the growth of the economy. The effect of these assumptions is that the faster rate of growth permitted by the imposition of import controls would lead to a *slower* rather than a *faster* rate of inflation. For this reason the CEPG attaches significantly less importance to the adverse reactions of the world financial community, and the consequent need for exchange controls, than is the case here; though it is fair to add that in the early 1980s the economic programme of Britain's Labour Party, which was influenced by the Cambridge Group's work, did attach great importance to reimposing and strengthening the exchange controls which the Conservative government had abolished in 1979.

2 A further assumption made by the Cambridge Economic Policy Group is that because domestic manufacturers—at any rate in Britain—appear to determine their prices on the basis of a fixed percentage mark-up on average unit costs, they will not take advantage of import controls to raise their prices to domestic consumers. This assumption is a particularly contentious one.
3 In practice, of course, this may not be so, since some people may genuinely prefer no street lighting and lower taxes, or may feel that they are bearing an unfair share of the cost. But this is an ineluctable problem in any collective decision-making process.
4 Over the two-year period 1971 to 1973 OECD industrial production rose by 16 per cent.

CHAPTER 8

1 See for example Denison, 1967.
2 Reported in *Financial Times*, 10 November 1982.
3 Reported in *Financial Times*, 13 December 1982.
4 See for example Jenkins and Sherman, 1979.
5 For a variety of views on these issues, see Friedrichs and Schaff (eds.), 1982.
6 For a discussion of these relationships in the British context, see Kaldor, 1982.
7 In some OECD countries, of course, cars are produced by firms that are nationalised rather than owned by private shareholders (e.g. British Leyland in Britain and Renault in France). However this is irrelevant to the argument in the text, which is concerned essentially with the distinction between goods and services which are marketed, and goods and services which are provided free of charge by central and local government, and financed out of taxation.
8 For example in 1982 the All-Party Select Committee of the House of Lords estimated that in Britain the annual cost of an unemployed person to the Treasury, in terms of social security benefits and lost tax revenue, was about £5,000 (Report on Unemployment, HL, 1982, 142, p. 51).
9 Wilkinson, 1973.

CHAPTER 9

1 See for example Bury, 1920. According to Bury, 'the doctrine of Progress ... is now, even should it ultimately prove to be no

more than an *idolum saeculi*, the animating and controlling idea of western civilisation' (p. vii). He argues that the London Great Exhibition of 1851 was regarded not just as a record of material progress, but as an indication that humanity was on its way to a better and happier state (p. 331). By the 1870s and 1880s 'the idea of Progress was becoming a general article of faith' (p. 346).

2 On pp. 134–6. The evidence is reviewed in Easterlin, 1974, and Simon, 1974.

3 See for example Cole and others, 1973, and Beckerman, 1974.

4 In his Introduction to *The No-Growth Society*, Olson makes clear his own scepticism about the calls for a cessation of economic growth, referring to the economist's instinctive re-action: 'surely the desire for a more wholesome environment calls for a change in the composition of output entailing more expenditure on environmental improvement and less use of pollution-intensive goods and productive processes, rather than a ukase against growth itself' (p. 1). At the same time, he agrees that ' the advantages, disadvantages, and other properties of a society with little or no economic growth demand serious attention, however one views demands for an immediate halt to economic growth' (p. 3). In *Beyond Boom and Crash* and other books, Heilbroner examines the way that tightening environmental constraints might be expected to spell the end of the capitalist system.

5 Carbon dioxide in the atmosphere acts rather like the glass of a greenhouse, letting in solar radiation but absorbing longwave radiation coming from the earth's surface and re-radiating some of it back. The effect is to raise the earth's surface temperature.

6 Dasgupta and Heal, 1979, Chapter 7.

7 Hotelling, 1931.

8 Changes in the prices of minerals and fossil fuels over time are sensitive to the precise period chosen for examination — they were in fact unusually low in 1931 because of the depression; and not all exhaustible resource prices move in the same way. In broad terms, however, one would have expected, given positive real interest rates for much of the period, and increasing productivity in manufacturing industry, that there would have been quite a significant rise in the price of exhaustible resources in relation to the price of manufactured goods. This does not appear to have happened: if anything, raw material prices have fallen in relation to the price of manufactures. One explanation of this would be that extraction costs are both a relatively large proportion of market price, and have been falling over time. But

another, perhaps more plausible, explanation would be that economic theory which predicates the operation of competitive markets is not very good at explaining or predicting what happens in the real world.

9 Dasgupta and Heal, 1979, Chapters 6–8.
10 For a discussion of this problem see Dasgupta, 1982, Chapter 5.
11 I.e. an approach which postulates that people are asked to choose an equitable distribution of income from behind a 'veil of ignorance'—not knowing their own position in the income distribution (Rawls, 1972).

CHAPTER 10

1 Many of the facts and figures on which this chapter is based are derived from *Energy in a Finite World: Paths to a Sustainable Future*, a report by the Energy Systems Program Group of the International Institute for Applied Systems Analysis (Ballinger Publishing Company, Cambridge, Massachusetts, 1981). This report summarises the findings of what is probably the most thorough and comprehensive study of the global energy outlook that has yet been conducted. Only the most important specific page references are given in the text. Another major source is Gerald O. Barney (Study Director), *The Global 2000 Report to the President of the US: Entering the 21st Century*, Vol. I: *The Summary Report* (US Council on Environmental Quality). Page references are to the Pergamon Press edition, 1980.

2 BP *Statistical Review of World Energy*, 1981, p. 4. The price refers to Arab light crude.

3 BP, 1981, p. 4. In *The Limits to Growth*, it was predicted that if petroleum consumption continued to grow at an annual rate of 3.9 per cent, known global reserves would be exhausted in twenty years—i.e. by 1990 (Table 4, p. 58).

4 The writing—or some kind of writing—had been on the wall for a year or two. The Tehran Agreement, signed in 1971, and purporting to fix oil prices for the next five years, was in fact breached within a year; and 1972 and the first half of 1973 saw increasing pressure from the producing countries for participation in the concessions held in their countries by the oil companies, and for further price increases to take account of Western inflation.

5 Dasgupta and Heal, 1979, pp. 442–3.

6 Calculations derived from *National Institute Economic Review* (NIER), May 1982, p. 89, and BP, 1981.

7 For example Sheikh Yamani, Saudi Arabia's Minister of Petroleum, envisaged little rise in real oil prices throughout the rest of the 1980s (*Financial Times*, Survey of World Oil Industry, 2 December 1981).

8 Odell, 1981.

9 Reported in *Financial Times*, 10 June 1981. A pessimistic view about future oil supplies was also taken, a year later, by the director for group finance of British Petroleum, who stressed that 'no really large new accumulations of oil have been found anywhere in the world since the 1960s, despite greatly increased exploration effort' (reported in *The Guardian*, 14 July 1982).

10 See note 1.

11 IIASA, 1981, pp. 134 and 145–7.

12 *Global 2000* (see note 1), p. 175.

13 IIASA, 1981, p. 110.

14 *Global 2000*, p. 81.

15 *Global 2000*, pp. 141–4.

16 Estimates made by American National Academy of Sciences, quoted in *Global 2000*, p. 83.

17 IIASA, 1981, pp. 107–8; OECD, 1982, p. 9; *Global 2000*, p. 83.

18 Brown et al., 1979, pp. 46–8.

19 Commoner, 1976, pp. 105, 117.

20 Cook, 1981, p. 16.

21 Commoner, 1976, p. 102. Commoner's figure of 130 million pounds appears to relate to the US alone.

22 Commoner, 1976, p. 103.

CHAPTER 11

1 Particularly noteworthy was 'A Blueprint for Survival', a call for an end to economic growth endorsed by thirty-three eminent people, most of them scientists, and published in Britain in the January 1972 edition of *The Ecologist*.

2 IIASA, 1981, p. 88.

3 Brown, 1979, p. 36.

4 IIASA, 1981, p. 151–2.

5 A successful test was carried out on the Tokamak Fusion Reactor at Princeton, New Jersey at the end of 1982. Nevertheless, not until 1986 at the earliest was this machine expected to produce more energy than it consumed; US Department of Energy officials have said that 'barring a sharply intensified fusion research program, commercial fusion power may not be

available for at least 50 years, if ever' (quoted in *International Herald Tribune*, 30 December 1982).

6 IIASA, 1981, p. 140. A terawatt-year per year (TW yr/yr) is 10^{12} watt-years per year, and represents a convenient way of expressing *rates* of energy supply or use (see IIASA, 1981, p. 5).
7 IIASA, 1981, Table 8–10.
8 Brown, 1978, p. 113.
9 Reported in *International Herald Tribune*, 30 December 1982.
10 Conroy et al., 1982.
11 Reported in *Financial Times*, 17 May 1982 and 1 October 1982.
12 The seriousness of the problem may be masked for a while by the fact that at present much of the carbon dioxide released into the atmosphere is absorbed by the oceans. But if there comes a time—as some observers expect—when the oceans' ability to absorb carbon dioxide rather suddenly reaches saturation point, the build-up of carbon dioxide in the atmosphere could then become very rapid (OECD, 1982, p. 11).
13 BP, 1981, pp. 28–9.
14 *Global 2000*, p. 2.
15 *Global 2000*, p. 157.
16 *Global 2000*, p. 38.
17 OECD, 1982, p. 43.

CHAPTER 12

1 Chekhov, *Uncle Vanya*, translated by Elisaveta Fen, Penguin Classic edition, 1959, p. 223.
2 The widespread fall in inflation rates in the early 1980s seemed to owe little to the direct causal relationship between the money supply and prices claimed by monetarists (in Britain, to take an example, the increase in the money supply—sterling M3—in 1980–81 was over 20 per cent; but two years later the inflation rate was not the 15–20 per cent which mainstream monetarist models would have predicted, but around 6–7 per cent). The fall in world inflation owed far more to the high and rising level of unemployment and the high and rising number of bankruptcies which, compounded and spread around the world by the normal multiplier processes and the deflationary responses of the international financial community, were the indirect effects of monetarist policies. These effects naturally induced workers to moderate their wage demands and employers to toughen their bargaining stance, with a correspondingly favourable impact on

labour costs and hence on prices. The other major factor at work was the collapse of world commodity prices (excluding oil), which by 1982 were at their lowest level, in real terms, for more than thirty years (*World Development Report 1982*, figure 3.6). A reversal of the rise in unemployment, and a recovery of the world economy, is likely in turn to reverse both these favourable influences on inflation.

Sources and References

ALIBER, ROBERT Z., (ed.), *The Political Economy of Monetary Reform* (Macmillan, 1977).

BARNET, RICHARD J., and MÜLLER, RONALD E., *Global Reach: The Power of the Multinational Corporations* (Simon and Schuster, New York, 1974).

BECKERMAN, WILFRED, *In Defence of Economic Growth* (Jonathan Cape, London, 1974).

BERGSTEN, FRED C., HORST, THOMAS and MORAN THEODORE H., *American Multinationals and American Interests* (The Brookings Institution, Washington D.C., 1978).

BP *Statistical Review of World Energy 1981.*

BROWN, LESTER R., *The Twenty-Ninth Day* (W.W. Norton, New York, 1978).

BROWN, LESTER R., FLAVIN, CHRISTOPHER and NORMAN, COLIN, *Running on Empty* (W.W. Norton, New York, 1979).

BRYANT, RALPH C., *Money and Monetary Policy in Interdependent Nations* (The Brookings Institution, Washington D.C., 1980).

BRYANT, RALPH C. and KRAUSE, LAWRENCE B., 'World Economic Interdependence' in Joseph A. Pechman (ed.), *Setting National Priorities: Agenda for the 1980s* (The Brookings Institution, Washington D.C., 1980).

BURY, J.B., *The Idea of Progress* (Macmillan, London, 1920).

COLE H.S.D. and others, *Thinking About the Future: A Critique of 'The Limits to Growth'* (Chatto and Windus, 1973).

COMMONER, BARRY, *The Poverty of Power* (Jonathan Cape, London, 1976).

CONROY, CZECH, FLOOD, MICHAEL and GORDON,

DAVID, *Eclipse of the Sun? The Future of Renewable Energy Research in Britain* (Friends of the Earth Ltd., London, 1982).

COOK, ROBIN, *No Nukes!* (Fabian Society, London, July 1981).

COOPER, RICHARD N., *The Economics of Interdependence: Economic Policy in the Atlantic Community* (McGraw Hill, New York, 1968).

CORDEN, W.M., *Inflation, Exchange Rates and the World Economy* (Clarendon Press, Oxford, 1977).

DASGUPTA, P.S. and HEAL, G.M., *Economic Theory and Exhaustible Resources* (James Nisbet and Cambridge University Press, 1979).

DASGUPTA, P.S., *The Control of Resources* (Basil Blackwell, Oxford, 1982).

DENISON, EDWARD F., *Why Growth Rates Differ* (The Brookings Institution, Washington D.C., 1967).

DEVARAJAN, S. and FISHER, A.C., 'Hotelling's 'Economics of Exhaustible Resources': Fifty Years Later', *Journal of Economic Literature*, March 1981.

DORFMAN, ROBERT and DORFMAN NANCY S., (eds.), *Economics of the Environment* (second edition, W.W. Norton, New York, 1977).

DOW, J.C.R., *The Management of the British Economy 1945–60* (Cambridge University Press, 1964).

EASTERLIN, R.A., 'Does Economic Growth Improve the Human Lot?' in P.A. David and M.W. Reder (eds.), *Nations and Households in Economic Growth* (New York, Academic Press, 1974).

FRIEDRICHS, GUNTER and SCHAFF ADAM, (eds.), *Microelectronics and Society: For Better or Worse. A Report to the Club of Rome* (Pergamon Press, Oxford, 1982).

The Global 2000 Report to the President of the US: Entering the 21st Century. Volume I: The Summary Report (US Council on Environmental Quality 1980; Pergamon Press, 1980; Penguin Books, 1982).

HANSEN, BENT, *Fiscal Policy in Seven Countries 1955–65* (OECD, 1969).

HEILBRONER, ROBERT L., *An Inquiry into the Human Prospect* (W.W. Norton, New York, 1974).

HEILBRONER, ROBERT L., *Beyond Boom and Crash* (W.W. Norton, New York, 1978).

HIRSCH, FRED, *Social Limits to Growth* (The Twentieth Century Fund, 1976; Routledge and Kegan Paul, 1977).

HOTELLING, HAROLD, 'The Economics of Exhaustible Resources', *Journal of Political Economy*, April 1931.

House of Commons Treasury and Civil Service Committee, Session 1979–80, *Memoranda on Monetary Policy* (HMSO, London, July 1980).

International Energy Agency, *Energy Conservation: The Role of Demand Management in the 1980s* (OECD, Paris, 1981).

International Institute for Applied Systems Analysis (IIASA), Energy Systems Program Group, *Energy in a Finite World: Paths to a sustainable Future* (Ballinger Publishing Company, Harper and Row, Cambridge, Massachusetts, 1981).

International Monetary Fund, *World Economic Outlook* (IMF, Washington D.C., April 1982).

JACKSON, DUDLEY, TURNER, H.A. and WILKINSON, FRANK, *Do Trade Unions Cause Inflation?* (Cambridge University Press Occasional Paper 36, 1972).

JAY, PETER, Article in *The Times*, 15 April 1976.

JENKINS, CLIVE and SHERMAN, BARRIE, *The Collapse of Work* (Eyre Methuen, London, 1979).

KALDOR, NICHOLAS, *The Scourge of Monetarism* (Oxford University Press, 1982).

KENNEDY, M.C., 'Employment Policy: What Went Wrong?' in Joan Robinson (ed.), *After Keynes* (Basil Blackwell, Oxford, 1973).

KEYNES, J.M., *Essays in Biography* (Macmillan, London, 1933). (The page reference in the text is to the 1972 Royal Economic Society edition.)

KINDLEBERGER, CHARLES P., *The World in Depression 1929–1939* (Allen Lane The Penguin Press, London, 1973).

KINDLEBERGER, CHARLES P., 'Dominance and leadership in the international economy: exploitation, public goods and free rides' in *Hommage à François Perroux* (Presses Universitaires de Grenoble, 1978).

LLEWELLYN, DAVID T., *International Financial Integration* (Macmillan, London, 1980).

MATTHEWS, R.C.O., 'Why Has Britain Had Full Employment Since the War?', *Economic Journal*, September 1968.

MCCRACKEN, PAUL and others, *Towards Full Employment and Price Stability* (OECD, June 1977).

MEADOWS, D.H. and others, *The Limits to Growth* (Earth Island, London, 1972).

MISHAN, E.J., *The Costs of Economic Growth* (Staples Press, 1967; Penguin Books, 1969).

ODELL, PETER R., 'Lower Oil Prices: Dangers to the North Sea', *Lloyds Bank Review*, October 1981.

OECD, *From Marshall Plan to Global Interdependence: New challenges for the industrialised nations* (OECD, Paris, 1978).

OECD, *Economic and Ecological Interdependence* (OECD, Paris, 1982).

OLSON, MANCUR and LANDSBERG, HANS H. (eds.), *The No-Growth Society* (The American Academy of Arts and Sciences, 1973 and The Woburn Press, London, 1975).

PAISH, F.W. and HENNESSY, J., *Policy for Incomes* (Institute of Economic Affairs, 1964).

PAQUET, GILLES, (ed.), *The Multinational Firm and the Nation State* (Collier-Macmillan, Canada, 1972).

PHILLIPS, A.W., 'The Relationship between Unemployment and the Rate of Change of Money Wage Rates in the U.K., 1861–1957', *Economica*, November 1958.

PLIATZKY, LEO, *Getting and Spending* (Basil Blackwell, Oxford, 1982).

RAWLS, JOHN, *A Theory of Justice* (Oxford: The Clarendon Press, 1972).

SAMPSON, ANTHONY, *The Money Lenders* (Hodder and Stoughton, London, 1981; Coronet Books, 1982).

SCITOVSKY, TIBOR, *The Joyless Economy* (Oxford University Press, 1976).

SIMON, J.L., 'Interpersonal Welfare Comparisons Can Be Made', *Kyklos*, 27, 1974.

SOLOMON, ROBERT, *The International Monetary System, 1945–1976: An Insider's View* (Harper and Row, New York, 1977).

SOLOMON, ROBERT, (with GAULT, ANNE), *The Economic Interdependence of Nations: An Agenda for Research* (The Brookings Institution, Washington D.C., June 1977).

SOLOW, ROBERT M., 'The Economics of Resources or the Resources of Economics' in Dorfman and Dorfman, 1977.

THUROW, LESTER C., *The Zero-Sum Society* (Basic Books, New York, 1980; Penguin Books, England, 1981).

TUGENDHAT, CHRISTOPHER, *The Multinationals* (Eyre and Spottiswoode, London, 1971; Random House, New York, 1972).

WILKINSON, R.G., *Poverty and Progress* (Methuen, London, 1973).

World Bank, *World Development Report 1982* (World Bank, Washington D.C., 1982).

Abbreviations and Glossary

Externalities   The effects on other people of a person's (or firm's, or government's) action, of which no account is taken when the decision to engage in the action is made. A *positive* externality will benefit other people, a *negative* externality will harm them.

Free rider   Someone who benefits from the provision of a public good (*q.v.*) but pretends he does not and successfully avoids helping to pay for it.

GDP   Gross domestic product, or the value of the total output of an economy. *GNP*, or gross national product, is GDP *plus* net income from abroad. US and IMF statistics tend to quote GNP data, European and OECD (*q.v.*) statistics GDP data; but for most practical purposes the two concepts are used interchangeably.

Gilts   Gilt-edged securities, or government bonds, whose redemption value is guaranteed by the government.

OECD   Organisation for Economic Co-operation and Development (see note 4, page 171).

PSBR   Public Sector Borrowing Requirement, or the amount that a government in Britain needs to borrow each year in order to finance the difference between its expenditure and its revenue. For practical purposes, it can be regarded as the same thing as the budget deficit.

Public goods   Goods or services the consumption of which by one

187

person does not reduce their consumption by other people; and which—if provided for one person—other people cannot readily be excluded from consuming. Examples are street lighting and broadcast weather forecasts. Because public goods cannot easily be charged for, they normally have to be provided by governments, and financed out of general taxation.

Sterilisation   Under a fixed exchange rate regime, an inflow of foreign exchange into a country will lead to an increase in its domestic money supply, and an outflow to a reduction in it. If the government does not want these foreign exchange flows to affect the domestic money supply in this way, it will *sterilise* or neutralise them, selling securities in the open market in order to offset the expansionary effect of a foreign exchange inflow, or buying government securities in order to offset the contractionary effect of a foreign exchange outflow.

Supply elasticity   The extent to which the supply of a good increases in response to an increase in the demand for it, as reflected in a rise in the price offered for it.

Index

DATE DUE

APR 1 3 1990